# FAITH AND JUSTICE

*The Social Dimension*
*of Evangelization*

# FAITH AND JUSTICE

## *The Social Dimension of Evangelization*

**Jean-Yves Calvez, S.J.**

Translated by
John E. Blewett, S.J.

THE INSTITUTE OF JESUIT SOURCES

ST. LOUIS 1991

This book is a translation of

Jean-Yves Calvez, S.J.,
*Foi et Justice: La dimension sociale de l'évangélisation,*
published by Desclée de Brouwer, Paris, 1985.

Number 12 in Series II:  Modern Scholarly Studies about the Jesuits
in English Translation

3700 West Pine Boulevard
St. Louis, MO  83108
Tel: 314-652-5737
Fax: 314-652-0810

Library of Congress Catalog Card Number 91-75164
ISBN 0-912422-49-1

# CONTENTS

Numerous members of religious congregations of men and women, along with many bishops, priests, and lay Catholics, as well as many others who are not members of the Church, have some knowledge of, or at least have heard mentioned, a Jesuit document entitled *The Service of Faith and the Promotion of Justice* or, in shortened form, *Faith and Justice*. This document was produced in 1975 by the Thirty-second General Congregation of the Jesuits. (A "congregation" is nothing other than what other religious congregations call their general chapter.)

## The Mysterious Decree Four

First of all, many have had occasion to perceive the impact of this document on the Jesuits themselves. If they have attended meetings with Jesuits, they may have heard them frequently mention a mysterious Decree Four. For example, about a year ago a French non-Jesuit priest returning from a meeting of the Jesuit Mission among Workers remarked how often he had been fascinated by constant references to Decree Four. "What is this new gospel of the Jesuits about which I am ignorant?" he wrote. He lost no time in laying hands on a copy of the document which we are now discussing.

Jesuits use the word "decree" to refer to every decision taken by general congregations, those concerning juridical matters as well as those dealing with more general orientations. In effect, every general congregation has the equivalent of a Decree 4 in its proceedings. But the words "Decree 4" have taken on extraordinary significance, becoming almost equivalent to a proper name. It is possible that that title will remain even after the Thirty-third General Congregation, which took place in September and October 1983 and certainly has its own Decree 4 among its decisions. This will indicate how wide have been the repercussions of *The Service of Faith and the*

*Promotion of Justice* among Jesuits, including those who did not greet it with enthusiasm. For there were some in that category also.

## The Events of the Years 1980 to 1983 in the Society of Jesus

Another reason for the interest in what we will call Decree 4 is the feeling that there is a connection between it and the extraordinary events in the life of the Society in recent years, most especially its relations with the Holy Father.

Everyone was able to learn even from the world press that in 1980 Father Arrupe, Jesuit superior general since 1965, had all but decided to call a general congregation and present his resignation as superior general by reason of his age and the onset of deep fatigue. Pope John Paul II, however, told him to put off acting upon that decision.

Concerned about certain aspects of Jesuit life, the Pope did not wish the congregation to take place before these matters were clarified. In the first months of 1981, he had two lengthy discussions with Father Arrupe on the subject, and he anticipated others.

Two events intervened before the discussions could be resumed: on May 13 the attempt on the life of the Pope in St. Peter's Square, and on August 7 the sudden illness of Father Arrupe resulting from a cerebral thrombosis. It soon became clear that, even should he survive the most acute phase of his illness, Father Arrupe would remain badly handicapped and would not be able to function again as superior general. He had, indeed, already appointed a vicar-general to assure governmental continuity. In October, however, the Pope stepped in and nominated Father Paolo Dezza, S.J., as his personal delegate to handle the preparations for the general congregation. Bringing about the clarification desired by the Pope was the matter at issue.

That clarification, as a matter of fact, took place rapidly—at the end of February 1982—when the Pope confidentially discussed the whole situation with all the provincial superiors of the Society at a meeting convened by Father Dezza. Shortly after, the latter transmitted to the entire Society what the Pope most wanted. When the

Pope was satisfied with Jesuit efforts to enter into his views, he permitted the congregation to be convoked on December 8, 1982, after a delay of two years.

The following steps are a matter of record: the opening of the congregation on September 1, 1983; its acceptance of the resignation of Father Arrupe; the election on September 13 of his successor, Father Peter-Hans Kolvenbach; and the return to normal government following this unusual period.

Now, as was widely conjectured, there was a connection between Decree 4 of General Congregation 32 and these events, a connection, certainly, to be clarified and accurately determined; a very real connection, but not merely one of simple causality.

It is worth the effort, then, to understand Decree 4 and the history of its development, and then to evaluate its meaning. The matter in question, to be sure, is a page in the history of a particular religious order. It is not out of place, however, to place the whole matter before a much wider public, especially since, as we will soon see, at least some of the problems that we will meet are not peculiar to a single religious order. They were and are questions for the whole Church. Perhaps the reflections contained in this book will throw some light on these questions for others as well as for Jesuits.

## Promotion of Justice, a Demand of Service of the Faith

Since the text itself of *The Service of Faith and the Promotion of Justice* is probably not well-known, we will incorporate it in the Appendix of this book. A few necessary remarks should be made in this introductory chapter to indicate at least its most striking aspects.

There is, first of all, the introductory statement: "The mission of the Society of Jesus today is the service of the faith, of which the promotion of justice is an absolute requirement. For reconciliation with God demands the reconciliation of people with one another."[1]

Next is the paragraph in which the key word "decision" ("choice," "option") appears:

> From all over the world where Jesuits are working, very similar and very insistent requests have been made that, by a **clear decision** [option, choice] on the part of the General Congregation, the Society should commit itself to work for the promotion of justice. Our apostolate today urgently requires that we take this decision. . . . Hence, fidelity to our apostolic mission requires that we propose the whole of Christian salvation and lead others to embrace it. Christian salvation consists in an undivided love of the Father and of the neighbor and of justice. Since evangelization is proclamation of that faith which is made operative in love of others, the promotion of justice is indispensable to it. (no. 28 [77], emphasis added)

These statements should be seen in connection with some other important ones which occur in another decree of General Congregation 32, entitled *Jesuits Today* and dealing with the question of Jesuit identity. "To be a companion of Jesus today," we read, is to "engage, under the standard of the Cross, in the crucial struggle of our time: the struggle for faith and that struggle for justice which it includes" (Decree 2, no. 2, [12]). Then, "the way to faith and the way to justice are inseparable ways. It is up this undivided road, this steep road, that the pilgrim Church must travel and toil. Faith and justice are undivided in the Gospel which teaches that 'faith makes its power felt through love.' They cannot therefore be divided in our purpose, our action, our life" (no. 8 [18]).

---

[1] *Our Mission Today: The Service of Faith and the Promotion of Justice,* Decree Four of the Thirty-second General Congregation of the Society of Jesus, in *Documents of the 31st and 32nd General Congregations of the Society of Jesus,* ed. John W. Padberg, S.J. (St. Louis: The Institute of Jesuit Sources, 1977), no. 2 [48]. All of the citations from General Congregations 31 and 32 are taken from this volume, which will itself be cited as *Documents.*

## Action on Structures, Social Involvement, and Solidarity with the Poor

Accordingly, Decree 4 involved the question of a significant though not exclusive attention to action on structures.

> In a world where the power of economic, social and political structures is appreciated and the mechanisms and laws governing them are now understood, service according to the Gospel cannot dispense with a carefully planned effort to exert influence on those structures. . . . The struggle to transform these structures in the interest of the spiritual and material liberation of fellow human beings is intimately connected to the work of evangelization. This is not to say, of course, that we can ever afford to neglect the direct apostolate to individuals, to those who are the victims of the injustice of social structures as well as to those who bear some responsibility or influence over them. (nos. 31, 40 [80, 89])

The members of General Congregation 32 recommended, as a consequence, a notable "social involvement" and a clear "solidarity with the poor." These are its words:

> Our faith in Christ Jesus and our mission to proclaim the Gospel demand of us a commitment to promote justice and to enter into solidarity with the voiceless and the powerless. This commitment will move us seriously to verse ourselves in the complex problems which they face in their lives, then to identify and assume our own responsibilities to society. (no. 42 [91])

Furthermore, it insisted:

> Our Jesuit communities have to help each of us overcome the reluctance, fear and apathy which block us from truly comprehending the social, economic, and political problems which exist in our city or region or country, as well as on the international scene. . . . We cannot be excused from making the most rigorous possible political and social analysis of our situation. . . . Nothing should excuse us, either, from undertaking a searching discernment into our situation from the pastoral and apostolic point of view. From analysis and discernment will come committed action; from the experience of action will come insight into how to proceed further. (nos. 43f [92f])

With a much further involvement in mind, the congregation included the following words: "Any effort to promote justice will cost us something. Our cheerful readiness to pay the price will make our preaching of the Gospel more meaningful and its acceptance easier" (no. 46 [95]).

The promotion of justice, the congregation added in clarification, was not to be merely "the choice of a few Jesuits only. It should be a characteristic of the life of all of us as individuals and a characteristic of our communities and institutions as well" (no. 48 [97]).

In the same way the decree called for solidarity with the poor and, even more explicitly, "with those who live a life of hardship and who are victims of oppression." This should not be the task of a few but should be "a characteristic of all of us as individuals and a characteristic of our communities and institutions as well" (no. 48 [97]). "Alterations" are needed "in our manner and style of living." The statement continues: "The same questions need to be asked in a review of our institutions and apostolic works" (no. 48 [97]). Jesuits are aware that sometimes their personal backgrounds, their studies, and the circles in which they move often "insulate" them from poverty and even from the "simple life and its day-to-day concerns" (no. 49 [98]).

> It will therefore be necessary for a larger number of us to share more closely the lot of families who are of modest means, who make up the majority of every country, and who are often poor and oppressed. Relying on the unity we enjoy with one another in the Society and our opportunity to share in one another's experience, we must all acquire deeper sensitivity from those Jesuits who have chosen lives of closer approximation to the problems and aspirations of the deprived. (no. 49 [98])

Finally, in a rather lively tone, Decree 4 again invited Jesuits to a reexamination of their choices regarding solidarity and commitment:

> Where do we live? Where do we work? How? With whom? What really is our involvement with, dependence on, or commitment to ideologies and power centers? Is it only to the converted that we know how to preach Jesus Christ? These are some of the questions we should raise with reference to our membership individually, as well as to our communities and institutions. (no. 74 [123])

## Involvement

An important part of the program of Decree 4 concerned what it called involvement: abolishing the distances separating one from another, meeting people, getting to know them better. It was not a question merely of injustice but of nonbelief as well. The congregation states:

> Too often we are insulated from any real contact with unbelief and
> with the hard, everyday consequences of injustice and oppression.
> As a result we run the risk of not being able to hear the cry for the
> Gospel as it is addressed to us by the men and women of our time.
> A deeper involvement with others in the world will therefore be a
> decisive test of our faith, of our hope, and of our apostolic charity.
> Are we ready, with discernment and with reliance on a community
> which is alive and apostolic, to bear witness to the Gospel in the
> painful situations where our faith and our hope are tested by
> unbelief and injustice? Are we ready to give ourselves to the de-
> manding and serious study of theology, philosophy and the human
> sciences, which are ever more necessary if we are to understand
> and try to resolve the problems of the world? To be involved in the
> world in this way is essential if we are to share our faith and our
> hope, and thus preach a Gospel that will respond to the needs and
> aspirations of our contemporaries. (no. 35 [84])

## Originality of the Decree

Decree 4 spoke about a good number of other important points: "inculturation" of the faith and Christian life; encounters with nonbelievers; renewal in the use of the Spiritual Exercises of St. Ignatius; more generally, "service of the faith," which provides the context for promotion of justice. The document also underlined characteristics of the promotion of justice that would make it truly a part of evangelization. The newness of Decree 4 is also evident in the option which the Society of Jesus made to commit itself with determination to the promotion of justice, and in the corollaries of that option: action directed toward structural change, solidarity with the voiceless and powerless, with the poor and victims of in-justice, as well as involvement with them.

On the other hand, one should not conclude that Jesuits had been strangers to the field of justice and inactive in the promotion of it. They had indeed been active there in different ways, especially through a notable contribution to the social apostolate and to the defense of the rights of oppressed people in Asia as well as in Latin America. Active, indeed, for many a year, as a matter of fact. Recall the Reductions of Paraguay or Father Lievens's notable efforts in the nineteenth century to defend the *adivasis* of Ranchi in northern India when they had been despoiled of their lands. From now on, however, more was at stake, and something else envisaged; namely, the promotion of justice was to become a dimension of all Jesuit works, and the service of the faith was to be regarded as integrally linked with the promotion of justice. "Service of the faith" and "promotion of justice" are together described as "**the** integrating factor of all our ministries; and not only of our ministries but of our inner life as individuals, as communities, and as a world-wide brotherhood" (D. 2, no. 9 [19], emphasis added).

### The Contents of This Work

Decree 4 was indeed new, and it is still far from having produced all its effects. Jesuits, consequently, should speak very modestly about it. With confusion, even, seeing how little they have as yet accomplished.

It would seem helpful at this point to try to give an outline of this book.

■ First, we will offer **the history of Decree 4** and explain how and in what context it appeared and what course it followed during the critical period from 1975 to 1983.

■ Then we will make clear its **theological underpinnings** by trying to determine what is now accepted, following more than one controversy.

■ Third, we will situate the fundamental choice of Decree 4, first in its relation to **the Church's total task of evangelization** and then within the purposes of the Society of Jesus.

■ Finally, we will examine some very **concrete aspects and problems** raised by certain of its elements: action on structures, political involvement, oneness with the poor, and insertion.

Decree 4 came into existence at a difficult time; one could say, in fact, that it was tossed on a stormy sea for several years. In particular, the actions of three successive popes (Paul VI, John Paul I, and John Paul II) to which we have already referred and to which we shall return are all among the elements of that "storminess." Today, finally, it is possible to point out what has been achieved and where we are on solid ground. It is widely known that Decree 4 was confirmed by General Congregation 33 in the fall of 1983. The reader will understand better in what precise sense this is true after reflecting on the contents of this book.

❖ PART I ❖

# HISTORICAL ELEMENTS

# Chapter One

# THE QUESTION OF JUSTICE AFTER THE
# SECOND VATICAN COUNCIL

D ecree 4 of General Congregation 32 is clearly not an isolated event. To understand it better and to measure its impact, we should recall what was beginning to happen after the Second Vatican Council (1962–65). A new and very intense concern for justice developed, which soon began to manifest itself in large sectors of the Church.

## *At the Council*

The council itself foreshadowed this phase of history through its willing spirit of dialogue and cooperation with all, and through its insistence on the value and meaning of every human undertaking within the plan of salvation itself. This was a decisive point, for without it the council could not have given so much importance to the furtherance of justice. It would have been especially difficult to link this concern so closely with faith and evangelization. "Throughout the course of the centuries, men have labored to better the circumstances of their lives through a monumental amount of individual and collective effort. To believers, this point is settled: considered in itself, such human activity accords with God's will."[1]

Of even greater importance was the fact that questions of justice appeared in different conciliar documents and—of greater significance still—questions of injustice and injustices. The council recog-

---

[1] *Gaudium et spes (The Pastoral Constitution of the Church in the Modern World)*, in *The Documents of Vatican II*, ed. Walter M. Abbott, S.J. (New York: Guild Press and America Press, 1966), 232, no. 34. All quotations from the Second Vatican Council are taken from this collection.

nized, first of all, that large numbers of people had become "clearly aware" of injustices and "unequal distribution" of this world's goods. Likewise among nations there are tremendous inequalities, and gaps between wealthy and poor only "grow more and more." Often, there is a kind of growth which seems to be unjust, characterized by "dependence, even in the economic sphere" (no. 9).

The council stated its conviction that "acts of injustice" were first among the various causes of division among people and that these gave rise to war.

> Many of these causes spring from excessive economic inequalities and from excessive slowness in applying the needed remedies. Other causes spring from a quest for power and from contempt for personal rights. If we are looking for deeper explanations, we can find them in human jealousy, distrust, pride, and other egotistic passions. (no. 83)

Further, it is "inhuman"—thus, even worse than "unjust"—"when government takes on totalitarian or dictatorial forms injurious to the rights of persons or social groups" (no. 75).

These are statements that one would not expect in conciliar documents. In themselves they indicated something new. The council further insisted that Christians fight for the furtherance of justice, and it specifically noted that priests should have a passionate love for it. "United with every man who loves and practices justice, Christians have shouldered a gigantic task demanding fulfillment in this world. Concerning this task they must give a reckoning to Him who will judge every man on the last day" (no. 93).

Finally, the Council expressed its desire "that some agency of the universal Church be set up for the world-wide promotion of justice for the poor and of Christ's love for them" (no. 90). Out of these efforts came Pope Paul VI's institution of the pontifical commission Justice and Peace, an entirely new name for a department of the Holy See.

### The Year 1968 and Those Following

However, despite its increasing awareness of injustice and its interest in justice and the advancement of it, we must add that Vatican Council II did not directly face the question which would count for so much in the following years, namely, the connection between promoting or struggling for justice and the Church's evangelizing mission itself. But this question quickly came to the fore. More so than ever before in the history of the Church, there was awareness, even widespread assertions that the concern for justice was directly linked with the proclamation of the Gospel. This was particularly true in 1968, when the question gained prominence in many countries. For Latin America, 1968 marked the years of Medellín and the Second General Assembly of the Latin American episcopate. One of that assembly's concluding statements was devoted to the question of justice, and this statement had immense effect. It can be said that at this moment an awareness of the injustices from which its people suffered crystallized in the general consciousness of the Church on the continent that contained the largest number of Catholics; moreover, the sense of the need to effect radical social change asserted itself. At the same time the conviction grew that the Church should assume a responsible position in this undertaking.

Concurrently, the "theology of liberation" was in the process of taking form. In 1971 there appeared the decisive work *Teología de la liberación: Perspectivas,*[2] from the pen of the man who can be considered the founder of liberation theology, Father Gustavo Gutierrez, a priest of Lima, Peru.

In Europe, 1968 was the time when small groups espoused revolutionary Christianity, whereas other groups—far more numerous—discovered the fact that human promotion and the search for justice were essential elements of Christianity. "Everything is political," many French people were then asserting. An ambiguous formula, indeed. The bishops were led to discuss the topic; and, the better to relate politics and faith, they took up the question at their 1972 meeting in Lourdes. At this meeting Msgr. Gabriel Matagrin presented an important paper, *Politics, Church, and Faith.*

In 1974 the French bishops took up the question again on an even larger scale, using a document of reflections prepared by its

---

[2] For an English translation of this work, see Gustavo Gutierrez Merino, *History, Politics, and Salvation,* trans. and ed. Sister Caridad Inda and John Eagleson (Maryknoll, N.Y.: Orbis Books, 1973).

permanent council and entitled "Forms of Liberation and Salvation Through Jesus Christ."[3] "There is no lack of success in the material, technical and perhaps spiritual realms," the bishops affirmed; "but perhaps never more than in our days are different forms of dependency and tyranny felt to be so threatening, nor have dangers so involved collective dimensions." In this context, they continued, "Christians openly welcome God's grace, and affirm their will to free themselves from various modern forms of captivity and oppression." Further, they said, "the liberation that Christians affirm in the name of the salvation which comes from Jesus Christ and of the mission guided by his Spirit is not without its political impact. [It] challenges society to organize itself anew in accordance with more evangelically human purposes." Clearly, the French bishops warned, the Church is not going to be counted with political forces and movements, nor are bishops or priests to have a role as "political or economic leaders," even when they are in union with socially disadvantaged groups. Above all, the Christian message "can never be tied up with cultural intrigues and socio-economic ideologies." Nonetheless, there is no lack of strong words of encouragement, already heard in Vatican Council II. "Christian eschatology," the bishops say, "is the foundation of the road of hope, along which the human person with his tasks and actions moves in history. It provides an anticipation of the kind of attainment of his objectives which he cannot expect from his own resources alone."

The same movement was observed in the neighboring country of Italy, where it led to the organization in 1976 of a very large meeting of the Italian church, on the theme "Evangelization and Human Promotion."[4]

---

[3] Permanent Council of the French Episcopate, *Les libérations des hommes et le salut en Jésus-Christ* (Paris: Le Centurion, 1974). The following quotations are taken from this source.

[4] Bartoletti et al., *Evangelizzazione e promozione umana: Riflessione biblico-teologico-pastorale* (Rome: Editrice AVE, 1976).

## *"Justice in the World" at the Synod of 1971*

This 1976 meeting in Italy followed Jesuit General Congregation 32, but prior to it other important developments took place in the universal Church. Especially significant was the third regular synod of bishops in 1971, which took up the question of justice in the world. The Synod fathers drew up their own conclusions under the title *Justice in the World,* which soon thereafter Pope Paul VI authorized to be published in their entirety. They were a continuation of the council and of *Populorum progressio,* his encyclical on development, and an echo, moreover, of the findings of Medellín.

It is worthwhile to recall some of the key phrases from the synod's documents, all too often forgotten. They call to mind that stage in the life of the Church.

> Listening to the cry of those who suffer violence and are oppressed by unjust systems and structures, and hearing the appeal of a world that by its perversity contradicts the plan of its Creator, we have shared our awareness of the Church's vocation to be present in the heart of the world by proclaiming the Good News to the poor, freedom to the oppressed, and joy to the afflicted.[5]

The bishops note especially, "Action on behalf of justice and participation in the transformation of the world fully appear to us as a **constitutive dimension** of the preaching of the Gospel, or, in other words, of the Church's mission for the redemption of the human race and its liberation from every oppressive situation" (no. 6).

The synod's more detailed analysis of injustice in the world is in itself very characteristic, and further on we will find frequent echoes of it in Decree 4 of the Jesuit general congregation. The world, in the words of the synod, is facing a "great crisis of universal solidarity." It gave this more precise description of the crisis:

> Never before have the forces working for bringing about a unified world society appeared so powerful and dynamic. . . . The paradox lies in the fact that within this perspective of unity the forces of

---

[5] *Justice in the World,* in *The Gospel of Peace and Justice: Catholic Social Teaching since Pope John,* presented by Joseph Gremillion (Maryknoll, New York: Orbis Books, 1976), 514, no. 5.

division and antagonism seem today to be increasing in strength. Ancient divisions between nations and empires, between races and classes, today possess new technological instruments of destruction. The arms race is a threat to man's highest good, which is life; it makes poor people and individuals yet more miserable, while making richer those already powerful; it creates a continuous danger of conflagration, and in the case of nuclear arms, it threatens to destroy all life from the face of the earth. At the same time new divisions are being born to separate man from his neighbor. Unless combatted and overcome by social and political action, the influence of the new industrial and technological order favors the concentration of wealth, power and decision-making in the hands of a small public or private controlling group. Economic injustice and lack of social participation keep a man from attaining his basic human and civil rights. (nos. 7–9)

The bishops continued as follows:

In the last 25 years, the hope has spread through the human race that economic growth would bring about such a quantity of goods that it would be possible at least to feed the hungry with the crumbs falling from the table, but this has proved a vain hope in underdeveloped areas and in pockets of poverty in wealthier areas. (no. 10)

There is in those last few lines an allusion to the criticisms, then quite frequent, of theories of development which were popular in the sixties. According to such theories, strong and widespread economic growth, especially in the industrialized world, would not fail to spread to developing countries, which in turn would be invited to make use of the same production-based formulas. "Developmentalist" theories, they were freely called by Latin Americans, who countered them with their own theories of "dependence," which had as a corollary a strategy of "liberation" from that dependence. As a matter of fact, it was hard to find many crumbs falling from the tables of the wealthy. A few "drops" of prosperity reached those in need, in contrast to what was expected as a result of a "trickle down" approach.

An evaluation excessively severe in some respects, because many countries of the Third World, including several in Latin America, did register very strong growth of their gross national product. What is all too true is that the wealth generated by this approach was badly distributed, and that large masses of the poor, both in cities and in rural areas, had no part in any true progress.

The synod of 1971 pursued its study of justice by denouncing a whole series of "voiceless injustices," situations of oppression and discrimination of all sorts, from those suffered by migrants and political prisoners to those of untruth in the world of communications and forms of "oppression encountered in the exercise of one's right to life" (380f). From this we can see that the synod did not have a narrow or exclusively economic view of injustice.

The year of the synod, 1971, is also memorable for Paul VI's *Octogesima adveniens*. Appearing in the spring, the letter marked the eightieth anniversary of *Rerum novarum*, the encyclical of Pope Leo XIII on the condition of workers. Paul VI's letter was much more concerned than the synod statement, *Justice in the World*, with problems of modern industrial societies. *Octogesima adveniens* very expressly and favorably responded to a request coming from Christians who had recently rediscovered the importance of politics. "The need is felt," asserted the Pope, "to pass from economics to politics," which "is a demanding manner—but not the only one—of living the Christian commitment to the service of others. Without, of course, solving every problem, politics endeavors to apply solutions to the relationships men have with one another."[6] In response to intemperate claims that "everything is politics," it is quite clear that the Pope described the limits of politics. "The domain of politics is wide and comprehensive," he stated, "but it is not exclusive. An attitude of encroachment which would tend to set up politics as an absolute value would bring serious danger."

On the other hand, the Pope took up the analysis of injustices within nations and, particularly, between nations, following the path already traced by *Populorum progressio*. On the subject of world trade, he wrote: "Relationships based on force have never in fact established justice in a true and lasting manner, even if at certain times the alternation of positions can often make it possible to find easier conditions for dialogue" (no. 43).

---

[6] *Octogesima adveniens,* in Gremillion, *The Gospel of Peace and Justice,* 507f, no. 46.

These words presaging what was to come with the rise of oil prices also warned of the limits, well understood, of that rise itself. The task at hand was to establish a true system "of greater justice in the sharing of goods, both within national communities and on the international level" (no. 43).

### Evangelization, Liberation, and Human Promotion

The synod of 1971 had a considerable impact on the Jesuit General Congregation 32. The synod of 1974, centered as it was on evangelization, did not fail to take up the same questions, which remained acute in various parts of the Church; namely, the relationship of evangelization to political and social liberation, to the struggle against injustices, and, more generally speaking, to "human promotion" or development. The synod preceded the congregation by only one month but did not directly influence it by a final statement, for it did not publish one. It was Paul VI who incorporated the work of the synod in his own synthesis, the apostolic exhortation *Evangelii nuntiandi,* which appeared only in 1975. But the points that the synod most insisted on were common knowledge even as they were being discussed, points which the Pope subsequently began to collect.

On the subject of liberation, at the center of Church concerns at that time, Paul wrote:

> It is well known in what terms numerous bishops from all the continents spoke of this at the last Synod, especially the bishops from the Third World, with a pastoral accent resonant with the voice of the millions of sons and daughters of the Church who make up those peoples. Peoples, as we know, engaged with all their energy in the effort and struggle to overcome everything which condemns them to remain on the margin of life: famine, chronic disease, illiteracy, poverty, injustices in international relations and especially in commercial exchanges, situations of economic and cultural neo-colonialism sometimes as cruel as the old political colonialism.[7]

---

[7] *Evangelii nuntiandi (On Evangelization in the Modern World)*, January 31, 1976 (Daughters of St. Paul edition), no. 30.

In this context, the theme of freedom from various forms of oppression, shameful situations, and injustices was expressly welcomed by the synod within the very framework of fundamental statements about faith and Christian spirituality:

> Between evangelization and human advancement—development and liberation—there are in fact profound links. These include links of an anthropological order, because the man who is to be evangelized is not an abstract being but is subject to social and economic questions. They also include links in the theological order, since one cannot dissociate the plan of creation from the plan of Redemption. The latter plan touches the very concrete situations of injustice to be combated and of justice to be restored. They include links of the eminently evangelical order, which is that of charity: how in fact can one proclaim the new commandment without promoting in justice and in peace the true, authentic advancement of man? (no. 31)

But the synod was clear too in its expression of concern about the tendency of some to reduce salvation, understood in a Christian sense, to temporal liberation or to "initiatives of the political and social order." Pope Paul continued his reflections on this topic as follows:

> But if this were so, the Church would lose her fundamental meaning. Her message of liberation would no longer have any originality and would easily be open to monopolization and manipulation by ideological systems and political parties. She would have no more authority to proclaim freedom as in the name of God. (no. 32)

He went on to say:

> The Church links human liberation and salvation in Jesus Christ, but she never identifies them, because she knows through revelation, historical experience and the reflection of faith that not every notion of liberation is necessarily consistent and compatible with an evangelical vision of man, of things and of events; she knows too that in order that God's kingdom should come it is not enough to establish liberation and to create well-being and development. (no. 35)

In brief, ambiguity was to be found in the use of the term "liberation" as employed by "ideologues, political groups and systems." The faithful, as such, should use the word in its full religious significance: "The liberation which evangelization proclaims and prepares is the one which Christ Himself announced and gave to man by His sacrifice" (no. 38).

Once again, we should point out that those statements of Paul VI occurred only after the Jesuit General Congregation 32 and its Decree 4, *The Service of Faith and the Promotion of Justice*. The Jesuit document, further, was more expressly centered on the theme of the promotion of justice rather than on liberation, even though this latter theme is not absent from the document. In any case, the Jesuit electors who gathered in December 1974 were strongly stimulated by the September-October discussions on evangelization at the synod.

### The Decisive Years

Looking back on all the events in the Church from 1968 to 1974, one is compelled to underline their originality: the framing of a new problematic only recently coming from Vatican Council II and its desire for a deeper penetration of Christianity into the concrete life of individuals and entire peoples. Discussion and debate were soon to crystalize around the word "justice" and the theme of liberation. At the same time all were being led to study anew the question of the relation between all forms of human activity and the Kingdom of God—especially activity on behalf of human promotion and its concomitant struggle for justice. Up for study, too, was the question of the relation of the promotion of justice to the service of the Gospel, the proper task and mission of the evangelizing Church.

In all history did Christians in general, theologians, and the Church itself ever concentrate such attention on the non-sacred, on the political and social, on issues of justice and injustice? Risks and real deviations were not lacking, to be sure; but there was the positive advantage of contributing better than ever to the question of integrating social life with the faith and Christian experience. We often remember the tumultuous aspect of that time; but we cannot forget the evidence of evangelical vitality: strong desires for life in harmony with the faith and for renewal of human society through the Gospel's message, new and fresh; the determination in a spirit of Christian youthfulness to break with the heavy burden of an all-too-frequent acceptance of and accommodation to unjust situations.

This was the setting for the Jesuit General Congregation 32, that assembly of the largest apostolically active religious order, facing head on the questions we have been considering. The electors were keenly aware of the widespread desire they represented because of Jesuit presence in a wide variety of pastoral endeavors in almost every country of the world. What positions would this group of men take with respect to new tendencies and problems? The question could not be without importance for the Church itself.

The Society of Jesus would make its response in Decree 4 of its General Congregation 32, and it is this statement we will be considering. However, before proceeding, we would like to look again at the setting in which Decree 4 appeared, but this time focusing upon the Society of Jesus. This is the concern of the next chapter.

# Chapter Two

# GENESIS OF DECREE 4

V atican Council II closed in 1965, the year when some of its most important documents received an affirmative vote; in particular, we recall the *Declaration on Religious Freedom* (*Dignitatis humanae*) and the pastoral constitution *The Church in the Modern World* (*Gaudium et spes*). For the Society of Jesus, too, 1965 stands as an important year; for, after a long generalate which began just after World War II and came to an end with the death of Father John Baptist Janssens in the fall of 1964, a new superior general was elected.

General Congregation 31, convoked for this election at the time of the council, when spirits were bubbling over, could not escape a long agenda concerned with reforms and orientations. It had to devote two sessions to its work, each about two and one-half months long: May 6 to July 15, 1965, and September 8 to November 17, 1966. It finished its work almost a year after the end of the council.

We must first point out that the congregation itself devoted much of its attention to Jesuit works and their apostolate, and to the orientation of both. Sixteen documents—some long, others brief—concerning the apostolate and its various sectors were eventually accepted. This does not include one particular decree—a very important document in itself—in response to the Pope's request that the entire Society of Jesus work with all its forces in opposition to atheism. There were decrees on the intellectual and scientific apostolate as well as on education; the work of spiritual formation and the apostolate in the field of mass media; ecumenism, missionary service, and, of course, the approach to nonbelievers. While involved with all these decrees, the members of the congregation spoke also of the **social** apostolate, without according it an especially important place. The main stress was on defining it well. There was, to be sure, quite an interesting insistence on the weight of "social structures" which "exert a very great influence on the life of man, even on his moral and religious life"; clearly, then, the problem of evangelizing these structures was raised. In the congregation's words, ". . . the social apostolate strives directly by every endeavor to build a fuller expression of justice and charity into the structures of human life in common. Its goal in this is that every man may be able to exercise a personal sense of participation, skill, and responsibility in all areas of community life" (GC 31, D. 32, no. 1 [569]). The "evangelization of social structures" meant breathing a more human spirit into them at least as much as it looked toward their "transformation," a term not yet used.

General Congregation 31, then, spoke of the social apostolate clearly and in a penetrating way, but above all it discussed it as a particular sector of apostolic action. The orientations given to this field by the congregation did not go beyond the directives laid out by the recently deceased general, Father John Baptist Janssens, who had vigorously promoted the social apostolate, including the founding of centers of social research and action throughout the entire Society of Jesus. He died, indeed, without having realized his desire to establish such a center in every province, but there were some twenty in operation at his death.

### The First Orientations Given by Father Arrupe

The activity of Father Pedro Arrupe, elected as Father Janssens' successor, centered more on setting orientations which would become the perspectives adopted by Decree 4. Not immediately, however. At first, as a matter of fact, his statements did not go beyond those of General Congregation 31, which we have just considered. He too seemed to treat the social apostolate especially as something separate. His interest in that area was indeed soon made clear in a lively manner; as can be seen in a message sent on July 24, 1966, to the centers of social research and action in Latin America.

A little later in the same year, however, he turned his attention to a more extended social commitment, one able to influence all forms of Jesuit apostolic activity.

In a letter of December 12, 1966, to Latin American provincials, he wrote:

     We must take into account the fact that socio-economic struc-
tures, by reason of their mutual interdependence, form a kind of
global social bloc or system. The intrinsic inadequacy of certain
fundamental structures for the establishment of a just social order
are mirrored in the global inadequacy of the existing system, which
is in contradiction to the Gospel.

     From this situation rises the moral obligation of the Society to
rethink all its ministries and every form of its apostolates to see if
they really offer a response to the urgent priorities which justice
and social equity call for. Even an apostolate like education—at all
levels—which is so sincerely wanted by the Society and whose im-
potance is clear to the entire world, in its concrete forms today
must be the object of reflection in the light of the demands of the
social problem.[1]

Similar attention, Father Arrupe went on, should mark "all the various
forms of the apostolate in Latin America."

In similar fashion, on November 1, 1967, he wrote to Jesuits of the
United States, describing the struggle against racial discrimination to be
carried on in all forms of their apostolic work. During a conference on April
2, 1968, he spoke of "the missions and social development." On a visit to
English Jesuits in January 1970, he treated the problem of the "underprivileged." While in Spain in May of the same year, he devoted an important
speech to Spanish Jesuits to "the social involvement of the Society." On the
other hand, it is true, in 1970 he spoke to the congregation of procurators—
an assembly of representatives of all the provinces held between general
congregations—about the social apostolate rather as an activity all by itself.

He delivered a very significant address on the question of justice at the
1971 synod of bishops, which would subsequently publish the document
*Justice in the World,* considered in our last chapter. As a follow-up of that
synod, responding to a request from the pontifical commission Justice and
Peace, he wrote an entire brochure entitled *Witnessing to Justice,* published
in 1972. It is a work which considers forms of action for justice in the
context of the evangelizing activity of the Church. More and more, then, a
concern for the promotion of justice took a conspicuous place among all
Father Arrupe's apostolic interests, but not to the exclusion of all else.

We must also cite his speech at Valencia, Spain, to alumni of Jesuit
educational institutions, delivered the following year, 1973. Entitled "Men
for Others," it carried a vigorous message, which disconcerted some in the
audience and prompted the president of the alumni association to resign.

     This kind of education goes directly counter to the prevailing
educational trend practically everywhere in the world. . . .

---

[1] *Acta Romana* 14, no. 6 (1966): 791.

Have we Jesuits educated you for justice? [Have you, our former students, been so educated?] . . . If the terms "justice" and "education for justice" carry all the depth of meaning which the Church gives them today, we have not educated you for justice.

. . . I think you will agree with this self-evaluation and with the same sincerity and humility acknowledge that you have not been trained for the kind of action for justice and witness to justice which the Church now demands of us. . . . [This] means that we have work ahead of us. We must help each other to repair this lack in us, and above all make sure that in the future the education imparted in Jesuit schools will be equal to the demands of justice in the world.

It will be difficult, but we can do it.[2]

In 1973 we approach General Congregation 32, which would be convoked in December 1974. The statements of Father Arrupe which we have recalled suffice in any case to help us understand how great an influence his personality was able to exert, as well as the orientations which he gave to the Society of Jesus, evident in the discussion and conclusions of that general congregation, particularly Decree 4.

## The Question of Justice in the Preparations for General Congregation 32

Another remark is in place here, one which may seem to conflict with what has just been said: The remote preparation for General Congregation 32, which consisted in a series of consultations from 1971 to 1973, did not really offer a preview of Decree 4. So it is worth recalling the tone which characterized the first preliminary steps, and then to pinpoint the moment which produced the modulation—we might say the change of tone—which led the congregation to make its characteristic choice.

The preparation for it began in 1971 when a document went out to the provinces including a collection of "those subjects to be taken up by the coming congregation." Those topics came in part from the

---

[2] See Pedro Arrupe, S.J., "Men for Others," *Justice with Faith Today: Selected Lettters and Addresses–II,* ed. Jerome Aixala, S.J. (St. Louis: Institute of Jesuit Sources, 1980), 125f.

provincial congregations and the congregation of procurators to which we have already called attention, all held in 1970. In this 1971 document there was only a simple allusion to "the social question." Moreover, the only remark about apostolates in general was this: "To determine better the apostolic service of the Society in a world which is secularized and a prey to tensions of development and under-development."[3]

In 1972 six working groups in different parts of the world (Brazil, East Asia, Southern and Western Europe, India, and North America) gathered to prepare a list of "propositions" on "the apostolic service of the Society today." (Similar groups were supposed to meet in Africa and Eastern Europe, but they were unable to do so.)

The question of injustice appeared in three of the six statements among the "major points needing consideration in the apostolic discernment of today." After the report on the collection of "propositions," the delegation from India said that it "saw in the abject and unjust condition in which large parts of humanity were living (deprived, in fact, of essential human rights) the most striking trait of today's world." It is, therefore, "impossible for a Jesuit, whether or not he is engaged in the social apostolate, not to make that problem the object of his prayer and constant concern." "The Society," the group insisted, "exists to respond to the most urgent needs."

The Indian group, in conclusion, proposed the following two statements for the study of the entire Society of Jesus:

1. First of all, our life should be a challenge to social realities characterized by sin, in our own Church and around it, and we should assure our brothers and sisters that we are not aligned with the forces and structures which perpetuate sin in our society.

2. In addition, with prudence but with no less courage, we should untangle the skein of hidden forms of sin which are the source of today's social injustices and demand, in the name of God, not only the palliative of social assistance, but the radical and rapid transformation accompanying a social, nonviolent revolution. To be an instrument of mediation and a catalyzing force in the struggle against all forms of enslaving sin is part of the Society's role.

---

[3] These and the following quotations are taken from unpublished materials available to the author.

For its part, the Asian working group said:

> To correct injustices, to free from oppression, and to teach men and women to use their strength for positive ends—all of this is to preach, by word and act, the Kingdom of God on earth. The actual divisions in society—person against person, one social class against another, nation against nation—make clear how very necessary is this apostolate of reconciliation. Those who enter the path of human development must necessarily struggle against those forces within themselves which tempt us to use hatred rather than love in the fight against social wrongs.

Finally, from Brazil came the following:

> 1. We must take our stand on the problems of freeing people from those forms of slavery which are brought on either by an excessive affluence or by dependence. Only a general mobilization of our forces in favor of the most needy will enable us to rediscover ourselves as the light infantry of the Church.

> 2. The majority of God's people are in a situation of extreme need; we should, therefore, reconsider how our forces are distributed, as the majority of Jesuits today are serving the minority, which has less need of us.

This convergence of concerns was significant. Along with them, however, many others are found in those documents of 1972; major points which also demanded attention in apostolic discernment were "unbelief and the urgent spiritual needs of large sections of humanity" (the most serious question, according to two groups); "aspirations to unity, especially among Christians" (ecumenism, that is; three groups insisted on this point); "the relation of both mission and dialogue as regards non-Christians (three groups). On the other hand, all the groups reached this overall judgment:

> There is no real need of new general orientations or of recommendations of particular forms of the apostolate. Before all else, we should seek the renewal of authentic, spiritual discernment concerning all apostolic works at every level of the Society, while directing close attention to the changes and new needs of the world.

There was still considerable distance between these statements and Decree 4, even though the reflections of several groups, especially those from the Third World, manifested a concern to assign an important place to questions raised by types of injustice, oppression, and various forms of "slavery" afflicting so many people.

Attention to justice, however, is found in a number of places in the collection of "propositions" or issues proposed for reflection by twenty groups similar to those we have just mentioned. These propositions were dispatched in 1972 to be discussed by Jesuits everywhere. Interestingly enough, the proposition concerning injustice and the struggle against its various forms was not one of those which captured the most attention. The *Synthesis of Reports* coming from the provinces in June 1973 manifested, on the one hand, agreement with that proposition, issuing from a desire for concrete, workable propositions (to avoid "beautiful but ineffective ideals") and, on the other, a significant disagreement. It even noted that a

> not-inconsiderable "minority" did not call for a strengthening of the proposition concerning justice, but instead criticized it as capable of deforming Jesuit apostolic work by turning it into a type of humanism or activism. Such criticisms caught "a stench of demagogy and Marxism" in it. Jesuits should be priestly rather than "sociologists" [*sociologues*]. . . . The General Congregation should declare that there is no pure and simple identification of work for God's kingdom or Jesuit apostolate in the Church with the struggle against poverty and injustice in the world. . . . The Gospel calls for conversion to the Father, not to sociology. Jesuits, return to the Gospel!

Polemic propositions, which foreshadowed others to follow after the congregation. In any case, the remote preparation for it did not lead one to foresee a favorable vote for a document like Decree 4.

## Requests from the Provinces on the Eve of the Congregation

The proximate preparation for the congregation turned out to be quite different, involving requests or "postulata,"[4] coming from the various provincial congregations held in the individual provinces during the spring of 1974. These postulata were not concerned with replies to or commentaries on the documents sent to the provinces by the preparatory committee. The initiative was entirely from the ground up, in the provinces. A considerable number of postulata dealt with the apostolate; but, in particular, a proportionally large number did not concern the "social apostolate"—as it was still re-

---

[4] [Translator's note: I will use the Latin word *postulatum* (pl. *postulata*) to refer to these official requests from the various provinces.]

ferred to—as much as the "social commitment" of the entire Society, "concern for the poor," the "priority" to be accorded these postulata, and, above all, "a choice of the Society for the promotion of justice."

The numerous requests concerning this last point were summarized as follows:

> That the General Congregation from the very beginning of its work make clear the Society's choice to further social and international justice so that all of its deliberations on our life and apostolate be inspired by that choice; . . . that the General Congregation decide and request of Father General that he set in motion a program of study and reflection on the part of the entire Society on questions concerning social and international justice.[5]

In sum, calls were made for "action for justice," including "international action," for which the Society was thought to be "particularly adapted." Further statements called in a particular way for action "to change the structures," to witness to justice by the example of one's way of living, to be in solidarity with the poor and victims of injustice, to "social responsibility" in the administration and use of the resources and goods of the Society itself, especially in what pertained to capital investments.

### A Model Postulatum

Readers will already have noticed on two occasions the call to "international" justice alongside social justice—a term that can hardly be found in Decree 4. Actually, if the question of "international justice" is so often found in the postulata of 1974, it is undoubtedly not because many Jesuits strongly desired to call explicit attention to that dimension; rather it is because a good number were inspired by a model postulatum coming from Mexico and widely disseminated in advance of the provincial congregations. This postulatum explicitly considered the "role of the Society in promoting international justice." This model was considerably modified and taken over by others, and the theme of "international"

---

[5] [Translator's note: This and the following quotations are taken from unpublished material available to the author.]

justice continued to occupy a prominent place in a fair number of postulata on the promotion of justice.

This model postulatum coming from Mexico was sent out on or about January 20, 1974. It is a sizable document—sixty-eight pages in its French version—with detailed statistical enclosures. To gauge its influence it suffices to compare its propositions with the summary of the postulata that all the members of the general congregation received, details of which we have just reviewed. They can be summarized as follows:

1. That the general congregation from the beginning of its labor so explicitly define an option of the Society as it faces problems of international justice that all subsequent deliberations concerning our life and apostolic mission in today's world be within the framework of that fundamental choice.

2. That the congregation approve a program of reflection for all Jesuits on problems of international justice and direct Father General to see to its execution.

## The Involvement of the General Congregation Itself

General Congregation 32 described itself on several occasions as inspired and urged on in its consideration of apostolates by the postulata from the provinces. Thanks to those postulata, it states, its gaze was fixed on "the vast expanse and circuit of this globe and the great multitude and diversity of people therein." These words are taken from the Spiritual Exercises, at the point where St. Ignatius directs the retreatant to see the Three Persons of the Trinity looking upon the human race and deciding to send the Son. "To the many requests received from all parts of the Society for clear decisions and definite guidelines concerning our mission today, General Congregation 32 responds as follows," it declared (D. 4, no. 1 [47]). More directly related to our subject was its statement that "from all over the world where Jesuits are working, very similar and very insistent requests have been made that, by a clear decision on the part of the general congregation, the Society should commit itself to work for the promotion of justice" (no. 28 [77]). It is clear beyond doubt that these words were a result both of the Mexican postulatum and of many others on the promotion of justice which were to a greater or lesser degree prompted by it.

There is no doubt, however, that it was the general congregation which committed itself, and it is easy to see clearly how different are postulata like those described above and Decree 4 as it was finally accepted. To underline only one point, we note that the postulata called in a special way for the congregation to take an **initial** position which would determine the way other questions should be handled. Beyond this, little more was called for than a program of reflection to begin throughout the Society after the congregation. The congregation really went beyond this, itself taking up the reorientation of the Society's apostolic works, urging at the same time that the provinces further its efforts by working out the meaning of the decree in various situations (no. 71 [120]).

Furthermore, we have already noted the difference between the concern for international justice so explicit in the postulata and the relatively modest and more balanced way it appears in Decree 4. In sum, we can say that the congregation more deeply probed the questions involved and so added considerably to the postulata. In fact, the congregation vigorously studied the questions proposed, adding a great deal to the postulata. At the very beginning it eagerly undertook its work, voting on the order of the day. When asked about the order in which to consider the forty distinct themes contained in the postulata, it placed the question of the promotion of justice in fourth place, reserving first place for the larger question of "criteria of our apostolic service today."

In a second consideration, however, the congregation went further. The first vote resulted in a selection of six points as priorities; but it accepted the suggestion that it take another vote to select "a priority of priorities." Another proposal was made to select both "criteria for our apostolic service today" and "promotion of justice" as the "priority of priorities." The congregation accepted this proposal, thus putting the "promotion of justice" in a new light.

The congregation, accordingly, decided something additional regarding the structure of its final document; namely, in its formulation the final document would not separate the question of the promotion of justice from that of the totality of apostolic service. The close relationship of the two themes was, however, not a foregone conclusion. Actually, two commissions had already been set to work, and they presented their conclusions independently of each other. When there was talk about putting the two themes together, some members expressed their reservations. The preferable course in their eyes was to treat the promotion of justice as **one** dimension of the entire apostolate, that is, as a particular sector. They were truly fearful that, if the two themes were to be united, the promotion of justice would come to occupy the whole field and appear to represent the totality of today's Jesuit apostolate.

On the other hand, however, it appeared to some that a separate treatment of the criteria for selecting apostolates and for propositions on the promotion of justice might become repetitious. This would surely be true if the promotion of justice were to be envisaged as an element of **every** apostolate. Some were clearly of the opinion that the justice theme should be integrated with every apostolate.

A more accidental reason led in the end to the unification of the two themes; namely, those charged with determining the criteria for every apostolate ran into unforeseen difficulty, stemming from the vastness and imprecision of their material. So members of the congregation sought a way out of the difficulty by trying to formulate in a single document everything involved in today's apostolate. The congregation further decided to unite the conclusions of the two commissions we have just considered with those of a third commission which sought to determine the meaning of "mission" itself and that of the mission of the entire Society **as a body.**

## Three Versions, Numerous Amendments

Out of the discussions came a considerable number of reports and three versions of the document, not to mention amendments. The document finally submitted to the vote was of great length, and the debates on it were quite long, representing in fact a great part of the congregation's work.

In the final vote those who were uncertain regarding the consequences of unifying the two themes—promotion of justice and criteria for the apostolate—proposed amendments intended to avoid the impression that the former represented the totality of the Jesuit apostolate. On the whole they were successful, so that the text which was accepted cannot in truth provide a foundation for that impression. This clash of opinions, however, makes clear where difficulties might arise in the interpretation and application of the decree.

There was broad agreement in the congregation both on the analysis of the state of the world and on the link in general between the service of the faith and the promotion of justice. On the other hand, opinions differed on the relative weight to be given to the promotion of justice in the global apostolate of the Society, as well as on the tasks to be taken up by each Jesuit. The diversity of particular situations partially explains this fact, but there was also a matter of doctrine. This helps to explain both the discussions that followed and even the papal interventions which we will soon consider.

At this point, we must repeat above all that the novelty of Decree 4 is not to be sought in the matter of service of the faith, but almost entirely in its statements on the promotion of justice. This was the theme which required the longest discussions and debates. It was on this theme that some of the strongest expressions were used, to the improvement of the decree. All in all, it was foreseeable that the treatment of justice in the decree would command the most attention and have the greatest impact.

A final point. We have spoken of the influence of the archetypal postulatum that came from Mexican Jesuits. Some have subsequently argued that Decree 4 was entirely due to Latin American influence. On the contrary, it seems clear that there would have been no such decree if the very lively Latin American sensitivity to questions of justice had not been notably combined with theological reflection coming more from European and North American sources. Further, the most active editors of the decree came from Northern Europe and Canada.

Delegates from other parts of the world, Asia, for example, saw in a general way the urgency of the struggle for the promotion of justice; but at the same time they were more concerned that the Society's work in evangelization, especially of non-Christians, should not slacken. Eastern Europeans likewise had their standpoint and were more concerned with the possible abuses of the idea of justice which might ensue. In the end, however, despite all differences the decree was almost unanimously accepted.

# Chapter Three

# THE YEARS 1975 TO 1978

A ccepted by affirmative vote in the spring of 1975 at the conclusion of General Congregation 32, Decree 4 would follow a truly extraordinary path in the following years and play a major role in the history of the Society of Jesus during this period. It was also to play a role in the relations between the Holy See and the Society from 1975 to 1983.

Since, in a certain sense, the Holy See became concerned about Decree 4 at the time of its final redaction, we will commence our discussion with that aspect of the document in order to sketch its history and repercussions.

In this chapter we will consider the period from 1975 to 1978, the latter year marking the end of a period. It was the "year of the three popes," notable for the death of Paul VI, the brief reign of John Paul I, and the election of John Paul II. At the same time it saw a congregation of procurators (elected representatives) of the Society of Jesus, its first important assembly following the general congregation and so an occasion for taking stock. The period from 1979 to 1983 we will consider in the next chapter.

## *Paul VI and Decree 4*

It is well-known, even by the general public, that General Congregation 32 experienced some difficulty in its relations with Pope Paul VI. It is appropriate, then, to look especially at the meaning of this, asking, for example, to what degree the wording of Decree 4 was at issue during this time of tension, and then to reply to that question. To give an overall answer right from the start, I would say that it seems unlikely that the Pope found the discussions on the commitment to justice to be a danger in themselves. How could it have been otherwise with the Pope who had issued *Populorum progressio* and *Octogesima adveniens?* His real fear was related to a "loss of identity" of the Society of Jesus because of certain reforms which, some thought, would lead it to lose its character as a "priestly" order, with all that that would entail for the apostolic works undertaken by Jesuits in their service of the Church. Decree 4, however, was involved insofar as one or other particular point in the discussions might seem to the Pope to confirm his basic fear.

We can examine certain documents preceding the general congregation in reference to the papal concerns; in particular, a letter which he addressed on September 15, 1973, to Father Arrupe and through him to all Jesuits, after Father Arrupe had informed him of his intention to convoke a general congregation. Considering the preparations of the congregation rather than the meeting itself, the Pope wrote:

> [The members of the Society] will have to rehearse with penetrating insight, a clear grasp of reality and a profound sense of duty, those principles of the spiritual and apostolic life which for centuries formed, as it were, the very structure that held the Society together, and which make it a most serviceable instrument for a pastoral, missionary, and educational apostolate involving cultural formation of the highest excellence.[1]

A bit further on he added the following:

> Nor are We ignorant of the fact that over the past few years in several parts of the Society—and it is by no means absent either from the life of the Church in general—certain tendencies have arisen of an intellectual and disciplinary nature which, if fostered and given support, could lead to serious and possibly irreparable changes in the essential structure itself of your Society. (18)

What the Pope had in mind with these words could be summed up thus: signs of excessive freedom in doctrinal matters; some harmful interpretations of Ignatian obedience and, indeed, of chastity as well. On the contrary, it would seem that no allusion was made to the new concern regarding the promotion of justice, a concern already manifested in certain parts of the Society. In short, however, the Pope was pointing to his misgivings about a fundamen-

---

[1] *Acta Romana* 16, no. 1 (1973): 17.

tal reform of the Society rather than about its adapting particular apostolic orientations—not that they were entirely excluded, as is clear from what follows in the letter.

In similar fashion, at the beginning of General Congregation 32, Paul VI delivered a long speech to all its members. Were his words indicating a program for the congregation? Certain members so interpreted his remarks. In any event, the Pope once again expressed his concerns.

He opened his talk as follows:

> [The present moment] demands of you more than a routine performance of your function: it demands an examination of the present state of your Society, one that will be a careful synthesis, free and complete, to see how it stands with regard to the difficulties and problems that beset it today. . . . to compare your identity with what is happening in the world and in the Society itself.

Then at length he posed these three questions to the Jesuits: "Where do you come from?" "Where are you now?" "Where are you going?"[2]

Showing a feeling of closeness to the Society, he sketched out the answers to his questions by appealing to Jesuit sources and tradition. So, he said, the first Jesuits from the very beginning clearly understood

> that the times required people who were completely available, capable of detaching themselves from everything and of following any mission that might be indicated by the Pope and called for, in his judgment, by the good of the Church, putting always in first place the glory of God: *ad maiorem Dei gloriam.* (523)

The Pope then specified this essentially mystical view: "You are religious. . . . You are, moreover, apostles. . . . And finally you are united with the pope by a special vow" (524–26). On each point he spoke precisely. He cautioned his listeners in strong language: "One must not call apostolic necessity what would not be other than spiritual decadence. . . . You are as well aware as we are that today there appears within certain sectors of your ranks a strong state of

---

[2] "Address of Pope Paul VI to the Members of the 32rd General Congregation," December 3, 1974, *Documents,* 520f.

uncertainty, indeed a certain fundamental questioning of your very identity" (528).

Responding to his own question "Where are you going?" the Pope told the Jesuits that they were to put into effect the *aggiornamento* called for by the council, but "in essential fidelity to the specific character of the Society and in respect for the charism of your Founder." He went on as follows:

> Perfection lies in the simultaneous presence of the two charisms—fidelity and service—without letting one have the advantage over the other. . . . Today the attraction of the second charism is very strong: the precedence of action over being, of activity over contemplation, of concrete existence over theoretical speculation. . . . [A]ll this could cause one to think that the two aspects of fidelity and love are mutually opposed. But such is not the case, as you know. People are never loved too much, provided they are loved only in the love and with the love of Christ. . . . [R]eadiness to serve can degenerate into relativism, into conversion to the world and its immanentist mentality, into assimilation with the world that one wanted to save, into secularism and into fusion with the profane. We exhort you not to be seized by the *spiritus vertiginis* (Is 19:14). (532f)

That the Pope did not wish these words to dissuade Jesuits from treating matters concerning their apostolic orientation is clear from the fact that he expressly presumes that such topics would be discussed. But he made a remark on this point which takes on its own meaning in respect to Decree 4.

> It will also be opportune to remember the need to make a proper **basic choice** among the many appeals that come to you from the apostolate in the modern world. Today—it is a fact—one notes the difficulty of making properly thought-out and decisive choices; perhaps there is a fear that full self-realization will not be achieved. Hence there is the desire to be everything, the desire to do everything and to follow indiscriminately all the human and Christian vocations—those of the priest and the lay person, those of the Religious Institutes and of the Secular Institutes—applying oneself to spheres that are not one's own. . . . But you have a precise vocation . . . and an unmistakably specific character in your spirituality and in your apostolic vocation. (534)

The members of the congregation heard these words with attention and perceived the emotion with which they were delivered. So, even though not all members tended to judge that the situation was as serious as it appeared to the Pope, they began to treat in depth questions relating to the very identity of Jesuits, their religious and community life, as well as prayer in the Society. They decided, nonetheless, as we have seen in the preceding chapter, to give priority to questions concerning criteria for the apostolate and, in particular, to what concerned the promotion of justice. That may have seemed to the Pope to be a different priority from what he preferred. In any event, the rumor, founded or not, began to spread that the Pope was concerned about the work of the congregation.

Some of its members were of the view that the best response to the existential questions concerning Jesuit identity would be to redefine their apostolic orientations in a way that would advance spiritual renewal. The Pope himself may well have desired that the questions of spiritual renewal be handled earlier and more directly. Subsequently, long discussions on the service of the faith and the promotion of justice took place in plenary session, while other questions were still in the hands of preliminary "commissions" or committees. By definition, one might say, the progress of work in committees or commissions is not as visible as the debates held in plenary session. There may have been some inner meaning found in the fact that work on other questions went much more slowly than did the discussions on the apostolate and promotion of justice.

If, however, there was reason to think that Paul VI was disturbed by the way in which the work unfolded, it was because relations between him and the congregation had worsened owing to another problem. A large number of Jesuits wanted to see greater equality among their members, particularly between priests and Brothers. Frequently this wish found expression in the proposition that all Jesuits should be eligible to pronounce the same four solemn vows, including that of obedience to the Pope in what concerned missions. The Pope himself, however, had made known his disagreement with this view through the Secretariat of State. His words were, " . . . such a change . . . seems to present grave difficulties which would impede the approval necessary on the part of the Holy See."[3] The congregation was not fully convinced that there

---

[3] "Letter of the Cardinal Secretary of State to Father General," December 3, 1974, *Documents,* 537f.

was no longer room for what it called "representation," that is, the presentation to competent superiors of difficulties that were perceived in connection with an order, even a very explicit one. So they proceeded to give their judgment, through an explicit vote, on the question of the possibility of a representation to the Pope. When informed of this step, he in turn was greatly displeased.

As a consequence of this, through a letter of February 15, 1975, the Pope firmly and finally confirmed his opposition to any change in the requirements for admission to the fourth vow concerning missions. But, in view of the context of the congregation's activity which we have outlined above, in his letter he did not confine himself to his remarks concerning the fourth vow; he also expressed his "doubt which arises in us from certain orientations and dispositions emerging from the work of the General Congregation."[4] He directed that very serious reflection be given to the matter and, further, requested that he be given the decrees decided on by the congregation before their publication (540). The Pope's knowledge of Decree 4 and of other documents under preparation undoubtedly led to this intervention, though, it is true, he did not give a more direct explanation of this action.

In its last sessions, then, the congregation tried to be even more attentive to the papal wishes, especially as expressed in his allocution of December 3, 1974.

### The Pope's Remarks at the End of the Congregation

Another phase began, then, as the congregation adjourned on March 7, 1975. A few days afterwards, the documents which it had accepted were sent to the Pope in accord with his wish. On May 2 they were returned "to be put into practice"; but they were accompanied by some remarks from Cardinal Jean Villot, the secretary of state, addressed to Father Arrupe in the name of the Pope. He indicated that, "while some statements merit total acceptance," the decrees included certain formulas which "are somewhat confusing

---

[4] "Autograph Letter of Pope Paul VI to Father General, February 15, 1975, *Documents,* 539f.

and could, because of the way they are expressed, give grounds for misinterpretation"[5] The first words just cited concerned the decree *On Our Mission Today: The Service of Faith and the Promotion of Justice,* and the declaration *Jesuits Today.* We have already shown that they were linked. The first remarks pertaining to them were:

> The promotion of justice is unquestionably connected with evangelization, but—as the Holy Father said in his closing remarks to the last Synod of Bishops in October of 1974—"Human development and social progress in the temporal order should not be extolled in such exaggerated terms as to obscure the essential significance which the Church attributes to evangelization and the proclamation of the full Gospel."[6] (547)

The second remark did not concern justice and evangelization in general but the role proper to Jesuits, or proper to priests and religious, in connection with the promotion of justice:

> [The Society of Jesus was founded] for a particularly spiritual and supernatural end. Every other undertaking should be subordinated to this end and carried out in a way appropriate for an Institute which is religious, not secular, and priestly. Moreover, we must not forget that the priest should inspire lay Catholics, since in the promotion of justice theirs is the more demanding role. The tasks proper to each should not be confused. (548)

The third remark concerned the collaboration of Jesuits with the local bishops in matters concerning the promotion of justice: "It is also helpful to recall that work for the promotion of justice should be undertaken in accord with directives drawn up by the local hierarchy and in consideration of the conditions peculiar to each region" (548).

As we read these concerns of Paul VI, some will certainly point out that there is no contradiction between them and the final text of Decree 4. True indeed. But it may also be said that Decree 4 did not particularly underline the points in question. In any event, we can better understand the points on which the Pope showed his concern if we relate his remarks on Decree 4 to his opposition to any change

---

[5] "Letter of the Cardinal Secretary of State to Father General, May 2, 1975, *Documents,* 546.

[6] The Pope repeated his earlier remarks, printed in *Acta Apostolica Sedis* 66 (1974): 637.

in the conditions Jesuits must meet before taking the fourth vow concerning special obedience to the Pope regarding apostolic missions.

This question about the fourth vow certainly can seem at first glance to have no relation to Decree 4, but actually the two were quite closely connected. The Pope did not explicitly explain in his letters to Father Arrupe the grounds for his opposition to the possibility that all Jesuits, non-priests included, might be eligible for the fourth vow. He merely commissioned Cardinal Villot to write on December 3, 1974, that the Institute of the Society reserves the fourth vow "to those religious who are priests and who have satisfactorily completed the required spiritual and doctrinal preparation" (537). But if we keep in mind the confirmation received from the Cardinal Secretary of State, we can readily say that the chief motive of the Pope was to keep the sacerdotal priesthood in the Society from being devalued. If he accepted the change which was envisaged, would the Society of Jesus not risk changing itself into a body made up indifferently of both priests and non-priests despite the fact that from its very beginning it was expressly "an order of priests" (ordo presbyterorum)? Further, might not there be serious consequences in the entire Church regarding the evaluation of the presbyteral priesthood? It was precisely on this point that a crisis had developed at the end of the sixties and the beginning of the seventies. Paul VI probably would have reacted under any circumstances as he did in order to protect an important mark of the traditional form of the Society; but, in view of the actual circumstances, he undoubtedly reacted more forcefully and emotionally.

If, on the one hand, we consider in this text the time and energy spent on Decree 4 during the congregation and, on the other, the lesser insistence on points such as those found in the papal remarks of May 2, 1975, we might suspect that the Pope probably had the impression that the Society of Jesus was in increasing danger of deviating from its fundamental character as a body of priests—the impression, that is, that there existed a tendency for it to turn into a secular institute; in other words, he sensed a tendency to accord too much weight to human promotion and social progress in contrast to the search for the Kingdom of God in its entirety.

## The Jesuit Reception of Decree 4

Against this background, we must point out developments in the Society of Jesus after the general congregation.

In the first place, it should be said that, when informed of the letter of May 2 from Cardinal Villot, Jesuits took very seriously the observations sent to them in the name of the Pope. At the same time they understood that the decrees had been returned "in order to be put into practice."

Beyond doubt there were hesitations, even resistance here and there. In light of the remarks made by the Pope, some simply doubted the validity of the orientations found in Decree 4. Others accepted the entire document, holding, however, that deficiencies were to be found in it. On the basis of correspondence received in 1975 on this subject from distinguished Jesuits engaged in the social apostolate, we may note the following:

> The document is very deficient in what concerns the substance of actions in favor of justice and, consequently, leads to many ambiguities in the interpretation that will be given it. . . . The concept of justice, as it appears in the document, lacks specificity; it appears to be the same as "socialism," that is, the equality of men and women in sharing of goods. This is a very important part of justice and undoubtedly the most urgent in many countries; but it is not the only one, even at the level of sociological analysis.[7]

Another view:

> There is much said in the decree about change of structures where they are unjust. But this is an impossibility unless we have at least a general understanding of possible alternatives. . . . As it is, many doubt today that a social teaching of the Church exists, or even that one is possible. With no model to propose as a substitute, the activists among us are going to be tempted to adopt the "Marxist" model (which really should be called "Leninist"), characterized by the dictatorship of the party, with all the present deficiencies of this model and the new forms of injustice flowing from it.

Another written observation was the following:

---

[7] [Translator's note: This and the following quotations are taken from unpublished material available to the author.]

As far as the most critical level of theological reflection is concerned, the document does not propose any norm of discernment which might guide us as we take action in the service of justice. Nothing is said about the tendency to identify evangelical action with political action in the strict sense of that term; such a temptation can be found frequently among Jesuits. It is not difficult to foresee that the decree will be joyously interpreted as justifying initiatives foreign to our mission.

There is no doubt, however, that the large majority of Jesuits welcomed the document, and it is impossible to think that their interpretations were as excessive as those we have just read. Some were enthusiastic about it and expressed their "great joy" about its orientations, which corresponded very well to the apostolic situation in which they worked. Others accepted these orientations quite readily, without understanding too well where they would lead.

In a good number of provinces in 1975 and 1976, there were meetings and assemblies for Jesuits to study and make their own the orientations of Decree 4, particularly what concerned the "promotion of justice," for this was the new element in that decree. Some provinces took up anew the whole range of their apostolic planning, devoting much time and work to this effort. Naturally, the promotion of justice held a place of distinction among the projects and programs resulting. This was true in Central America and in Bolivia, to mention some Latin American provinces; it was true also in French-speaking Belgium, Canada, and, somewhat later, Spain. Time and effort were devoted in several instances to sessions focused directly on the systematic analysis of the surrounding social reality.

### Social Apostolate: Jesuit Presence in Slums

The social apostolate, properly speaking, very soon became a focus of interest again, often in new forms. Several research and social-action centers devoted themselves more to action, for example, by helping to organize neglected people in rural areas, victims of flagrant injustices. Little by little new centers sprang up, clearly focused on influencing public opinion, as well as on denouncing unjust situations; this was true in North America, England, Ireland, and Australia.

In the years following the general congregation, small communities were started or developed among the very poor, especially in the huge slums adjoining metropolitan areas. This was especially true in the large cities of the Third World. In Europe missions to workers appeared where they had not been seen before.

It was only more slowly, on the other hand, that a concern for the promotion of justice spread to other forms of the apostolate. But here too there was no lack of effort following General Congregation 32. For example, directors of retreats tried to introduce this concern into their work, at least with chosen groups. A certain number at least of Jesuit-directed educational centers took the same road. In an address in 1976, Father Arrupe challenged those directly engaged in intellectual apostolates, forcefully stimulating them to a redirection of their work, or at least to a change in style in their activities, the better to contribute to the promotion of justice.

Three years after General Congregation 32, in 1978, Father Arrupe was able to say in an allocution opening the congregation of procurators:

> The struggle on behalf of faith and justice, understood in its proper breadth and depth, is without doubt one of the greatest changes taking place right now in the Society. Everywhere sincere efforts are under way to make this mission a reality. We are seeing less and less of that early fear, which arose in more than a few groups virtually everywhere in the Society, that the new emphasis was a deviation from the spirit of the Institute. Many are catching on to the significance of this mission and of the mind of the Church today.[8]

> The struggle for justice carries with it "solidarity with the poor." In spite of the difficulties that this solidarity can occasion, there is a perceptible growth in the Society of active interest in behalf of the poor and oppressed. Many Jesuits want to share really in the lives of the poor and seek some personal experience of injustice and oppression. (455, no. 9)

Putting into practice the orientations of Decree 4 also meant persecution and suffering for the Society, or at least for certain groups of Jesuits; and for some, even violent death. Father Arrupe observed that often "fidelity to the simple fulfillment of our mission

---

[8] *Acta Romana* 17, no. 2 (1978): 455, no. 8.

in difficult circumstances or in spite of the dangers peculiar to civil war has claimed its victims." As a matter of fact, there were some deaths because Jesuits remained at their post, close to the people, often to very poor people, during the struggle for freedom in Zimbabwe, during the unfolding of events which brought bloodshed in Lebanon since 1975, and during periods of disruption in Chad and India. Others were killed in certain Latin American countries because, albeit in unsophisticated ways, they explicitly stood up for justice as they carried out their pastoral ministry. At the 1978 congregation of procurators, Father Arrupe prepared a list of eleven victims, the price paid by the Society for direct or indirect orientation of its work in the spirit of Decree 4. There would be others in the near future.

Father Arrupe presented this balance sheet on the range of Jesuit apostolic works:

> During the past three years the Society's apostolate has been clearly changing, though in different ways and degrees in different Provinces.
>
> The main agent of this change has been Decree 4 which has brought about a distinct shift in our apostolate toward "the service of faith and the promotion of justice" both in education and pastoral work, social action, etc. The evaluation of our works, which is being carried out at the moment, is being done in the light of this priority. (463, no. 21)

### Clarifications, Interpretations: Role of Father Arrupe in These Years

At the same time, it is true, this picture did not lack its shadows. Included in this category were the "initial refusal" of some, to which Father Arrupe alluded, and the difficulties of others who were confused because their formation or pastoral methods had not accustomed them to take interest in social and political questions about which they understood nothing. We should also include the unauthorized interpretations found here and there which turned Decree 4 into a more or less total identification of the service of the faith with the promotion of justice—at least in our times.

Even after the conclusion of the congregation, Father Arrupe was visibly attentive to and persevering in the readjustment of choices, plans, and options so that this new approach—efforts made to promote justice—should find its place within the work of serving the faith, clearly and always the fundamental goal of the Society of Jesus. More frequently than not, he did this work by the spoken word. However, the official collection of documents of the Society (*Acta Romana Societatis Iesu*) contains traces of more than one written intervention similar to his spoken statements from 1976 through 1978.

Some of his letters concern the situation of men who were tempted to political action in the precise meaning of that term, in situations where Father Arrupe could not discern the exceptional character which might have justified them. Patiently he explained himself. He was also led to caution Jesuits concerning Marxism, underlining that the Church's preoccupation in this regard was not "a simple question of conservatism or immobility," but a reflection of the "progressive crumbling of the faith" found too often in the ranks of those who adopted Marxism even with those distinctions which they believed made it compatible with Christianity.

Other interventions of Father Arrupe concern the entirety of Decree 4 and its interpretation. For example, in 1976 he addressed a letter to a particular province which had sent him a document going well beyond that decree, intending to make it the guiding charter of that province. In response, Father Arrupe wrote as follows:

> I cannot approve an orientation for any particular province which is not entirely in accord with that given to the whole Society by the General Congregation. . . . Now in this document from your province everything is linked with injustice, while Decree Four gives a broader picture of things and recognizes not one cause alone but three causes of the present apostolic situation: namely, the fact that many people do not know Christ and it is very difficult to come close to them; then cultural change and secularization which presents a new challenge for the Faith; finally, injustice, which is particularly important for our mission of preaching the Gospel.[9]

In the letter in question, Father Arrupe notes that only "socio-economic" aspects of injustice are considered, but that they are not the whole story. The general congregation, he adds, "invites us to

---

[9] *Acta Romana* 16, no. 4 (1976): 1097f.

stand up to socio-economic injustice found not only in structures but also in the human heart itself and in the attitudes and tendencies which cannot be explained in terms of the economy" (1097).

Father Arrupe touched on other points in his letter: the option for the poor, who should not be confused with "those who claim to represent them"; likewise, the choice of socialism, which he depicts as not without ambiguity when one pretends to choose "a socialism which doesn't exist" in contrast to types of socialism which have effectively taken shape in history. Father Arrupe's essential objective is found in his efforts to make sure that the mission of the Society prescribed in Decree 4 will not be restricted. This mission does not consist solely in the promotion of justice, much less a limited version of it.

Addressing the congregation of procurators in 1978, Father Arrupe then took up each of the questions we have just noted (political activity not absolutely called for, the temptation of Marxism, the danger that some might reduce Decree 4 solely to the promotion of justice). He was quite clear and very forceful, certainly a sign that the problems were real, at least here and there.

Father Arrupe, indeed, went a long way with the concerns of his companions who were inclined to give priority to works involved in the struggle for justice or against human misery, but he also indicated their limits with great clarity. For example, he did not hesitate to pose the following formidable question:

> The Formula of our Institute describes spiritual ministries as principal means and those of corporal good works as subsidiary means. Today when so many necessities of the material order make themselves felt, and on a vast scale, service to alleviate them, well adapted in each case, can sometimes be of great value and, despite its rank as "subsidiary" should, so far as possible, be considered among the principal means of our apostolate. Did not Saint Ignatius provide shelter in his house for 400 unfortunates of Rome, not to mention the 3,000 others to whom he brought assistance? . . . Needs and their importance as Ignatian criteria for selection of works are in certain cases determined by the urgency [of the situation]. Service of the faith is certainly urgent in our secularized

pagan world, but all of us know that today there are millions who die of hunger.[10]

The solutions, he noted, should be discerned in each particular case. However, he added in a very significant way, "We cannot look on any means or any criterion of apostolic discernment as absolute—hunger, for example." "**Not even** hunger," Father Arrupe said in his desire to safeguard the priority of service of the faith, while fully aware of the dramatic character of certain situations where choice between the two had to be made. In every case, at any rate, where someone gave him the impression of being aware only of needs stemming from one or other form of injustice and of remaining insensitive to strictly spiritual needs, Father Arrupe reacted.

At the same time, at the 1978 congregation of procurators, Father Arrupe expressed his belief that a sizable part of the Society was slow to change:

> I don't deny that efforts are being made within our Society to reduce to practice the decrees of General Congregation 32. But if we look at the rhythm of change, the caution and fear, which in many places control and preside over the process of the necessary renewal, as well as at the lack of responsibility, especially on the part of institutions, we have the impression that we are still in the process of simply adapting to the demands of our time what we already have or what we have been doing. Often enough we do not dare to ask ourselves if that which we are not doing is more important than the works we are now engaged in, works which we ought to give up, for we cannot do everything. . . . We cannot let ourselves be penned in by apostolic structures which can turn into real traps because of an exclusive and absolute concern for today's needs. We should preserve our capacity for maneuver and transformations, all the time alert to the important human problems. (no. 6)

## Father Arrupe's Attention to Essential Spiritual Attitudes

Among all the activities of Father Arrupe during these years, we should keep in view as perhaps of still-greater importance his concern to go to the very roots of spiritual problems which both

---

[10] *Acta Romana* 17, no. 2 (1978), no. 13.

could and did arise in the process of applying Decree 4. He did this through two notable letters to his brethren, one dated November 1, 1976, on the integration of spiritual life and apostolate, the second, October 19, 1977, on availability for the apostolate. In his letter on integration, he wrote as follows:

> The 32nd General Congregation clearly supposes and expects that each Jesuit will have an integrated interior life that is both deep and personal. Indeed, the very "ideal" of an apostolic mission as it is presented by the 32nd General Congregation—and that in no way differs from the Formula of the Institute, which the Congregation sought to translate into contemporary terms—cannot be thought of, let alone expressed, without that integration.[11]

Father Arrupe invited the readers of the letter to question themselves about a spiritual life of total apostolic fruitlessness as well as about an apostolic life transmitting no spiritual experience.

In his letter of 1977 he presented availability as a test of integration.

> My question is: how can we know for sure if we are men who have reached a mature inner unity, really integrated, **for whom all experience of God is action for others and all action for others is such that it reveals to them the Father** and draws them closer to Him in affection and commitment?
>
> There is one way of knowing this and Saint Ignatius frequently refers to it. For him we are not ideal Jesuits, whatever our work, unless we remain permanently and joyfully "disposable," "men ready to be sent." And this holds for every moment of our life, even when we are undertaking with great enthusiasm a particular mission.[12]

This is a typically Ignatian way of acknowledging the absolute nature of God and the relative nature of everything else. In a word, it is to have faith.

As 1978 brought these first three years to an end, clearly the application of Decree 4 had only begun. Something, however, was really stirring. The tensions which had existed, it seemed, were on

---

[11] "Integration of Spiritual Life and Apostolate," *Acta Romana* 16, no. 4 (1976): 956.

[12] "Letter on Apostolic Availability," *Acta Romana* 17, no. 1 (1977): 137.

the decline. Unauthorized and excessive interpretations there were, but Father Arrupe with patience and perseverance responded by incessantly inviting all to fidelity to the entirety of Decree 4. He strove to strengthen that spirit of fidelity at its very roots, in the spirituality of one and all. The immense majority of Jesuits were very much alert to the remarks Paul VI made in 1975. Until his death in 1978, the Pope did not have anything new to say on this question.

# Chapter Four

## THE YEARS 1979 TO 1983

L et us look again at some of Father Arrupe's statements to the procurators in 1978. On the one hand, he said, "the exaggerations and unilateral views of those who interpret our mission in too 'horizontal' and 'politicized' a fashion are gradually giving way to a more balanced interpretation." On the other hand, he said, "the initial rejection [by some] has become weaker, and in a more relaxed atmosphere such Jesuits are trying to deepen, in a more serious and complete way, their understanding of the decrees and the spirit of the 32nd General Congregation." There was more and more acceptance that "the mission to struggle for the faith and for justice should affect the lives and works of all Jesuits and not be limited to a specific apostolate reserved for some."[1] There was a better understanding that in every apostolate integration was to be sought between service of the faith and promotion of justice.

### *Recommendations of Pope John Paul I*

Once the diagnosis had been made, it remained only to set out on the journey. At the very moment, however, when Father Arrupe was making his appraisal, the recently elected pope, John Paul I, was preparing to give a rather severe allocution to the procurators, whom he was to receive in audience. He died, however, on the eve of the day scheduled for that talk, but Father Arrupe requested and received a bit later a copy of the remarks which he had prepared.

Decree 4, or, rather, the way it was being put into practice, provided the background for certain statements contained in the papal allocution.

---

[1] *Acta Romana* 17, no. 2 (1978): 485, no. 8.

You well know and with reason are preoccupied by the great economic and social problems which humanity today is experiencing, problems which have so many connections with Christian life. But in trying to solve these problems, always know how to distinguish the tasks of religious priests from those that belong to the laity. Priests should inspire and animate the laity in the execution of their responsibilities, but they should not take their place and neglect their own specific task of actively evangelizing.[2]

A bit further on John Paul I called attention to "the spiritual and supernatural purpose [of the Society] to which every other activity is to be subordinated. This is to . . . be carried on in a way that is appropriate for a priestly, religious group."

These remarks echoed those of Pope Paul VI in 1975; if one wants to look at it that way, they contained nothing new. But that very fact meant that his successor shared his concern three years later, even while at the same time making clear his warm sympathy and even his great affection for the Society. From the Society he expected much. He recalled what Pope Marcelus II—who himself held office only a short time—said to St. Ignatius: "You bring people together and train them for combat; then we will put them to work."

### Pope John Paul II in His Turn

A year later, on September 21, 1979, John Paul II met for the first time with a group of Jesuit officials. The occasion was a meeting of the presidents of the conferences of provincials, gathered at the beginning of September for their annual meeting. Following in the steps of his two predecessors, he said, "Pay attention to the apostolate which is proper to an order of priests; be conscious about the sacerdotal character of your activity down to the most diverse and most difficult of your apostolic endeavors."[3]

Two and one-half years later, on February 27, 1982, four months after he had appointed a papal delegate to prepare the upcoming general congregation, the Pope spoke at great length to the Jesuit provincials convened for a meeting. Two important passages of his

---

[2] *Acta Romana* 17, no. 2 (1978): 214.

[3] *Acta Romana* 17, no. 3 (1979): 638f.

address which are connected with our subject we should single out. On the one hand, he praised the social work of Jesuit missionaries, while carefully defining that work in the following terms:

> While the principal object of their mission was to communicate the faith and the grace of Christ, they try at the same time to raise the human and cultural level of the people among whom they work and to further a kind of social life which is more just and more in accord with God's design; so history reserves forever a memory of the famous reductions in Paraguay.[4]

On the other hand, one passage was directly consecrated to the question of the promotion of justice. To provide the context for this remark, we should certainly point out that the Pope had already demanded the pursuit as well as the adaptation of different traditional forms of the Jesuit apostolate, along with involvement in the new domains of ecumenism and relations both with non-Christian religions and with nonbelievers. At this point he brought up a subject to which he wished to "draw their attention":

> In our days we feel with ever-growing urgency, the necessity of promoting justice in the evangelizing activity of the Church. If we keep in mind the real claims of the Gospel and, at the same time, the influence of social conditions on the practice of Christian life, it is easy to understand why the Church looks on the promotion of justice as an integrating part of its evangelization. (no. 8)

In this passage the Pope used certain words from Decree 4 itself and others from the 1971 synod of bishops. He also promptly reiterated the recommendations of his predecessors, making use of a long quotation from his own address to the priests of Rio de Janeiro.

> In this domain [of the promotion of justice], not everyone has the same function. In what concerns the Society, one should not forget that the necessary concerns for justice should come into play in conformity with your vocation as religious and priests. As I said on July 2, 1980, at Rio de Janeiro, "If it truly wishes to remain faithful to itself, priestly service is *par excellence* and essentially spiritual. This characteristic should be again underlined today in opposition to the manifold tendencies to secularize the priest's ministry by reducing it to a purely philanthropic function. The priest's service is not that of a medical doctor, social assistant, politician or labor leader. In certain cases perhaps the priest can provide these

---

[4] *Acta Romana* 18, no. 3 (1982): 725, no. 5.

kinds of service in substitution [for the laity], as in the past he has done in a remarkable way. Today, however, such services are provided in suitable ways by other members of society, while our priestly service ever more clearly and specifically is a spiritual one. It is in the world of souls, of their relations with God and their interior links with their peers that the priest has an essential role to play. It is here that the priest should offer his assistance to modern man. Surely, whenever circumstances so demand, he must also provide material help through the works of charity and the defense of justice. But, as I have already said, in the ultimate analysis, what is involved is a secondary service which should never lead us to lose sight of the principal service, which is to help souls discover the Father, open themselves to him and love him in all things." (no. 8)

Underlining his point by insisting upon it, the Pope continued:

The Second Vatican Council has highlighted the importance and nature of the lay apostolate and has called on the laity to play their part in the mission of the Church. But the role of priests and religious is different. They do not have to replace the laity and even less should they neglect the task which is specifically theirs. (no. 8)

In his letter of March 25, 1982, communicating to Jesuits a detailed account of the Pope's desires, Father Dezza, the papal delegate, for his own part placed the apostolate in first place and underscored the priestly character of Jesuit apostolates, understood, of course, in a broad sense in accord with Jesuit tradition. Then he returned to the characteristics of the work of promoting justice, in accord with the religious and sacerdotal finality of the Society. "One cannot approve certain tendencies to consider the promotion of justice no longer as a demand of the faith but as practically giving full expression to it."[5] Some Jesuits, then, were going beyond the words of Decree 4, which spoke of that work as an "absolute demand" of the service of the faith, not as its full and complete expression.

Moreover, the proper role of priests, as distinct from that of the laity, was described as follows:

In the economic, social and political field, the role of priests is to educate toward justice and social commitment, and to encourage lay people to carry out their duties fully without replacing them in these. The priest's role is to indicate christian principles concerning

---

[5] *Acta Romana* 18, no. 3 (1982): 792.

economic, social and political life; to denounce injustices, to exhort people to work for the improvement or reform of institutions; to expound the social doctrine of the Church, not so as to find solutions for concrete social and political problems, which is the task of lay people, but to help them reflect on the errors and dangers of a materialist capitalism and a marxist collectivism so as to avoid passing from one unjust regime to another equally unjust one, even though different in orientation and opposed in ideology.

Ours cannot take part in political parties or assume directly political positions save in really exceptional cases, approved by the Bishops and by Father General.

Finally, it is worth noting that among the causes of the social injustices suffered by so great a part of mankind not the least important are those which must be sought in men themselves, specially those who carry greater responsibilities, in their personal egoism, in their real interests not publicly declared. To remedy these injustices, it is certainly necessary to strive for a better social and political order, but it is no less necessary that such people should be reached by other efforts directed towards a religious and moral improvement of man himself. And this is precisely the specific role of the priest, directed towards men of different factions, tendencies and ideologies. In this way the priest, working through his priestly ministry in the service of the faith, makes an important contribution toward the promotion of justice. (793)

## More Intense Efforts to Apply Decree 4

In the course of 1978 and 1979 there was no slowing down of initiatives to put Decree 4 into practice. At the end of the congregation of procurators on October 5, 1978, Father Arrupe had strongly urged an intensification of this effort. He had warned against unauthorized interpretations, and he had again described the condition for making Decree 4 work: "a robust spirituality." By this he meant

a type of spirituality which one neither acquires nor maintains without continuing prayer which gives sense to our action. . . . Permit me to insist, even if my doing so violates all the rules of oratory. Our prayer must be more personal, deeper and longer, and then we must know how to share this sort of prayer with others.[6]

---

[6] *Acta Romana* 17, no. 2 (1989): 577, no. 28.

What was needed was authentic "fervor." With this word he recalled an expression of one of the early Jesuits, Nadal, a man who was close to St. Ignatius: "The Society is fervor." At the same time, however, what was really at stake was, in his view, a call to put Decree 4 into action more thoroughly and more courageously.

> When I consider the challenge which confronts us and which undoubtedly will become more serious and more demanding in the near future, I become persuaded that the response of the Society ought to be immediate, impassioned, born of our conviction that what is at stake here is an unavoidable imperative of our charism of service on behalf of the Church and the world—a service daring, generous, and devoted, beyond the restraints of personal or institutional immobility. (559, no. 3)

"As if nothing had been done up till now," replied the provincials of the United States, surprised at his insistent words. Actually, in the States as elsewhere there were initiatives, and not solely in the field of the social apostolate properly speaking. For example, the Jesuit Association for Secondary Education, the secretariat in support of Jesuit secondary schools in the United States, was trying to develop a dynamic way of bringing the dimension of the promotion of justice into education. One of its publications, which was also translated into French, was entitled *Sowing Seeds of Faith and Justice: The Formation of Christian Citizens.* The work was written by Father Robert Starratt of the Province of New England.

The Third General Conference of the Latin American episcopacy at Puebla at the beginning of 1979 provided a new stimulus to apostolic works for the promotion of justice on that continent. It also offered an occasion for Father Arrupe to provide further clarifications on the matter. In a letter of November 5, 1979, to the Latin American provincials following a meeting with them in Lima, he took the core idea from the document of Puebla. "The fundamental mission of the Church is to evangelize here and now and looking to the future." The largest number of Latin Americans have a deep faith, which it is necessary "to defend, educate and purify, as well as to spread."[7]

---

[7] *Acta Romana* 17, no. 3 (1979): 834–46.

On the other hand, Father Arrupe remarked that, confronted with the "injustices and inequalities" in Latin America, there was no escaping the need for a preferential option in favor of the poor, but—so far as the Society was concerned—"the economic and political" aspects of that option should not be put in first place. Jesuits should not center or "polarize" priesthood and the kind of religious life characteristic of the Society. Further, Jesuits had several ways—not only one—of contributing to the service of the poorest and the promotion of justice in their various apostolates. A year later, on December 8, 1980, Father Arrupe sent a series of directives and orientations to the Latin American provincials on the use of Marxist analysis. We will take up this matter again in a later chapter.

One significant initiative of Father Arrupe during this time concerned refugees. At Christmas time of 1979, while chatting one evening with his closest co-workers, he called to their attention the dramatic events concerning the boat people of Southeast Asia. Immediately the idea came to him of arousing the generosity of the Jesuit provinces best situated to undertake something on their behalf. The next morning he sent out a telegram to some twenty provinces in East Asia, India, Europe, and North America. "The response was remarkable," he noted several months later.

> Immediately offers of assistance were made, in men, materials and different resources of experience. Likewise, food, medicine, money. Further, more than one province tried by means of the media to influence their governments or private institutions capable of intervening. Offers came from Jesuits for pastoral work as well as for organizational work on behalf of the refugees.[8]

This was the starting point for many of the initiatives which stimulated the cooperation of Jesuits of very different countries to provide pastoral and moral assistance in the refugee camps of Thailand, Cambodia, Indonesia, Africa, and Central America. That work continues; to coordinate and support it, there is a small center in Rome, the Jesuit Refugee Service, and other centers as well on individual continents: in Bangkok for Southeast Asia and in Nairobi

---

[8] [Translator's note: Quotation taken from unpublished material available to the author.]

for Africa. It is an even more modest work than it may seem from this description, but meaningful nonetheless.

How many other initiatives there were of the same kind, greater or smaller in their outreach, primarily built up on the local level! For example, efforts toward reconciliation in Northern Ireland; in the Appalachians of the United States, an area well-known for its enduring depression; in Southern Italy, where for several years a new Jesuit community had been working in the area most affected by the great earthquake of 1980, which took a toll of three thousand lives.

In the spring of 1980, Father Arrupe realized a hope which had been maturing over the years—bringing together a group representing the Jesuit-Workers Movement in Europe. Again a significant initiative. The workers' mission, especially the component of priest-workers, had existed here and there, particularly in France, for more than thirty years. But by this move Father Arrupe gave it a blessing such as it had never received during those years. He published on April 16 the reflections inspired by that meeting. An important document, it was picked up by the press in several countries, beyond as well as within the Jesuit world. Indeed it appeared around the globe.[9]

Another point to be highlighted in the work of Father Arrupe was his conference early in 1981 entitled "Rooted and Grounded in Love," a title taken from Paul's Letter to the Ephesians. This occurred some months after the appearance of Pope John Paul II's encyclical on mercy. Father Arrupe had been working to prepare this conference even before the new encyclical was announced. He thought it necessary and urgent to return to the crucial question of the relation between the promotion of justice and charity in the fullest Christian sense of that term.

---

[9] *Acta Romana* 18, no. 1 (1980): 55–65.

## Lingering Unrest from 1980 to 1982

In this period, it is true, the insistent and repeated remarks of the popes in connection with Decree 4, its interpretation and application, along with the tensions that became apparent when in 1980 John Paul II postponed the general congregation, began to provoke some unrest, even consternation, here and there among those who had most heartily devoted themselves to making Decree 4 live. This aspect of the situation assumed more notable proportions after the papal intervention of October 1981.

So began a period of very intensive study, even though from time to time the suspicion arose that the papal doubt extended beyond abuses and unauthorized interpretations of Decree 4 and involved the decree itself. For example, some forty Jesuits from northern Latin America who were deeply engaged in the promotion of justice for some years met at the end of July 1982 at Jiutepec near Cuernavaca, Mexico, to evaluate the course they had taken. They carried on a study, indeed, a moving self-evaluation concerning the naiveté of certain positions which they had previously espoused. The participants came to a better understanding of how different are a truly apostolic approach to justice and the objectives of political parties, skilled in taking over organizations of people whom pastoral activity had originally gathered together.

Similarly, these men saw the importance of not undertaking social work detached from pastoral activity; they also saw more vividly the importance of a very clear spirituality in their work. Several of the participants, who for some time had yielded to excessively secularized views, came to a rediscovery of themselves. Thanks to all this, the participants in the meeting returned to their countries with a strong conviction of the importance of the work for the promotion of justice; but they also manifested the spirit of unrest we have just mentioned: Was it not the heart of Decree 4 which was held suspect by Church authorities?

## Appraisal, Confirmation, and New Starts in 1983

Decree 4, then, was at the center of reflective study in early 1983 when the provincial congregations convened to prepare for the general congregation scheduled for the fall. The largest number of postulata coming from these congregations concerned Decree 4. Clarifications were sought in light of all the problems which had arisen in the course of the application of that degree. But very often those calling for clarifications sought a confirmation of the decree itself in no uncertain terms, so as to dissipate the spirit of hesitation which was starting to spread more widely. Consequently, this was a task not devoid of difficulties.

General Congregation 33 took up this question at considerable length. It finally settled on a brief text, whose main points we will try to trace, because it settled the exact status of Decree 4 after the eight years we have just considered. The congregation had to state at the beginning that, all things considered, the appraisal of these years was a positive one, despite so many events that had succeeded in arousing anxiety. This position was taken in a context of both confidence and humility, as was noted in an introductory statement:

> We speak with confidence because we believe the options made by the 31st and 32nd General Congregations have been in conformity with the renewal inspired by Vatican Council II, the Synods of Bishops, and the teachings of recent popes. We speak with humility because we recognize the difficulties of the task and our own failures to respond wholeheartedly as religious priests and brothers to the challenge of integral evangelization in our modern world.[10]

The participants in the general congregation then described in some detail the positive aspects of the recent past.

> We have found these years an experience of grace and conversion for us as individuals and as a body. We have made serious efforts to address realistically the issues of atheism and indifference in our secularized world. Our religious life has been enriched by the opportunity to "labor with" Jesus in the greater service of the Kingdom. This closeness to the Christ of the Exercises has brought us closer to the poor with whom he identified himself. At times it has also brought us the persecution for his sake that he promised his followers. (no. 31 [34])

Then the participants listed with frankness what were considered to be the weak points or difficulties encountered.

---

[10] *Documents of the 33rd General Congregation of the Society of Jesus* (St. Louis: Institute of Jesuit Sources, 1984), D. 1, no. 29 [32].

Our reading of Decree 4 of GC 32 has at times been "incomplete, slanted and unbalanced." We have not always recognized that the social justice we are called to is part of that justice of the Gospel which is the embodiment of God's love and saving mercy. We have not learned to enter fully into a mission which is not simply one ministry among others, but "the integrating factor of all our ministries." We have found it difficult to understand the Church's recent emphasis on changing the structures of society, and what our proper role should be in collaborating with the laity in this process of transformation. (no. 32 [35])

So the congregation admitted to failures of several kinds, stemming especially from tendencies to reduce the concept of justice to a too human meaning or to give undue importance to the social apostolate or to fail to respect the proper roles of the laity.

General Congregation 33, therefore, admitted that there were tensions both within the Society and around it. Could it have been otherwise?

Some have at times emphasized in a unilateral fashion one aspect of this mission to the detriment of the other. Yet neither a disincarnate spiritualism nor a merely secular activism truly serves the integral Gospel message. Our experiences of recent years have made us increasingly aware that the more a Jesuit is exposed to situations and structures alien to the faith, the more he must strengthen his own religious identity and his union with the whole body of the Society as represented by the local community to which he belongs. (no. 33 [36])

A little further on the congregation tried to depict the situation of the world in terms where social and economic aspects narrowly understood did not obscure other factors.

Our contemplation of the world reveals a situation frequently hostile to the spreading of the Kingdom. The dominant ideologies and systems—political, economic, social and cultural—often prevent an adequate response to the most elementary aspirations of the human family at both national and international levels. A pervasive materialism and the worship of human autonomy obscure or obliterate concern for the things of God, leaving the minds and hearts of many of our contemporaries cold and empty. This both reveals and causes a profound crisis of faith that expresses itself in an atheism at once theoretical, practical and institutional. Lack of respect for a loving Creator leads to a denial of the dignity of the human person and the wanton destruction of the environment.

> Massive poverty and hunger, brutal oppression and discrimination,
> a frightening arms race and the nuclear threat: all offer evidence of
> sin in human hearts and in the core of contemporary society. (no.
> 35 [38])

Crises in faith and in values were evident as much as were those in social, economic, or political worlds, even while hunger, poverty, oppression, discrimination, and threats to peace remained sharply real. Nonetheless, the congregation listed signs of hope, often concerning overtly religious values, that were in evidence everywhere.

> Yet even as we consider these things, we observe other signs of
> the times that encourage us and give us hope. There is throughout
> the world a heightened sense of the solidarity of the human family
> and a rising consciousness, especially among the young, that con-
> ditions of misery and oppression cannot be tolerated. The Church,
> enlivened by Vatican Council II and expressing itself in new forms
> of community and parish life, is more and more engaged in works
> of peace and justice. Many of the world's religions and cultures are
> experiencing a new vitality; and there are indications of a growing
> search for meaning, sometimes expressed in more profound reflec-
> tion and in prayer. (no. 36 [39])

So in this context the congregation came to the heart of its position; namely, it eagerly responded to the calls the Pope directed to the Society, while at the same time confirming the orientations of General Congregation 32, especially those of Decree 4, orientations which the Society judged it would and should maintain.

Let us see, then, the summary of what the Pope asked for, as prepared by the congregation.

> As we opened the 33rd General Congregation, we heard Pope John
> Paul II tell us: "The Church today expects the Society to contribute
> effectively to the implementation of the Second Vatican Council."
> Moreover he repeated the mandate to confront the problem of athe-
> ism and cooperate in that profound renewal needed by the Church
> in a secularized world. He invited us to adapt our traditional apos-
> tolates to the different spiritual necessities of today, singling out
> the renewal of Christian life, the education of youth, the formation
> of the clergy, the study of philosophy and theology, research into
> humanistic and scientific cultures, and missionary activity. He
> encouraged us to pay particular attention to ecumenism, relations
> with other world religions, and the task of authentic inculturation.
> Finally the Pope, speaking of our apostolate, again drew our atten-

tion to the need to promote, within the Church's evangelizing action and in conformity with our priestly and religious Institute, "the justice, connected with world peace, which is an aspiration of all peoples." (no. 37 [40])

. . . [The congregation] readily receives the calls which the Pope has made to the Society, and commits itself to a full and prompt response. At the same time, we confirm the Society's mission expressed by the 31st and 32nd General Congregations, particularly in the latter's Decrees 2 and 4, which are the application today of the Formula of the Institute and of our Ignatian charism. They express our mission today in profound terms offering insights which serve as guidelines for our future responses:

- the **integration** of the service of the faith and the promotion of justice in one single mission
- the **universality** of this mission in the various ministries in which we engage
- the **discernment** needed to implement this mission
- the **corporate** nature of this mission. (no. 38 [41], emphasis in original)

The document goes on to strengthen this confirmation of intent by returning to the great need for "deeper involvement in the lives of people," necessity of cultural and social analysis, inculturation, the choice or "preferential love" for the poor, as well as other aspects typical of Decree 4.

At the same time the congregation expressed its belief that they misunderstood Decree 4 who thought that it provides reasons for looking with suspicion on the apostolates of education, the intellectual life, and research. "Of great importance among the ministries of the Society are the educational and intellectual apostolates." Jesuits involved in education "can exercise a deep and lasting influence on individuals and on society. When carried out in the light of our mission today, their efforts contribute vitally to 'the total and integral liberation of the human person leading to participation in the life of God himself'" (no. 44 [47]).

The concluding quotation in this statement, which presents a broad view of liberation, is, as a matter of fact, taken from Decree 2, no. 11 [21], of General Congregation 32. General Congregation 33 itself highlights the fact that, according to the Formula of the Institute of the Society, its mission is "to procure the integral salvation of the human race in Jesus Christ, beginning indeed in this life but finding its fullness in eternal life" (D. 1, no. 34 [37]).

At the end of this very lively period of history, we can then say that Decree 4 was upheld. But, to be sure, it was restored to its full sense: "the service of the faith and the promotion of justice understood **in an integrated manner**," as General Congregation 33 formulated it. It must be read, too, in line with the calls of the Pope, who is the principal source of the mission of the Society of Jesus. In these calls we can surely see that a request is made for increasing collaboration for the profound renewal of the human race as set forth at Vatican Council II.

On the other hand, the many controversies of this period were not fruitless. The same is true for the numerous papal interventions. The design of General Congregation 32 is thus seen as having clearer contours and a more precise shape.

It is possible, therefore, to seek to determine more clearly what is generally accepted today. By the Holy See as well, in view of its statements since 1975 and of the satisfaction which Pope John Paul II manifested with the outcome of General Congregation 33.

Our task in the following chapters is to examine more precisely the **achievements**: first, from a theological point of view as we look at the underpinnings of the doctrine which lies behind Decree 4; then, on the ecclesiological level or, if another formulation is preferred, from the viewpoint of the understanding of the mission of both the Church and the Society implied in Decree 4; finally, we can review in the same way the more particular parts of that achievement, such as the contribution to transformation of structures, solidarity with the poor, insertion, and political action.

✜    PART II    ✜


# THEOLOGICAL FOUNDATIONS

# Chapter Five

# "THE PERFECT JUSTICE OF THE GOSPEL"

The first question about Decree 4 often concerns the very meaning of the word "justice." So our first task is to determine what it means. "What kind of justice are you talking about?" asked some Jesuits, displeased or restless as General Congregation 32 came to an end and Decree 4 was promulgated.

What, as a matter of fact, did the members of the congregation want to say? For some readers, it seemed they were being asked to enroll in the service of a wholly worldly objective, of simple human justice; this, they thought, would constitute a betrayal of the proper work of the Society of Jesus. Did not "justice," as St. Paul used the term, have a very different meaning? Others thought that they were being presented with a kind of "justice" which was exclusively economic. In all of this, others asked, was "justice" not being contaminated by a Marxist meaning? There was still another question: the relationship between justice and charity. Now we must see some of the responses these questions received.

## Justice in the Human Family Is the Congregation's "Justice"

It is not possible, of course, to clarify all of these questions at one and the same time. So we begin with an important statement, but one which does not exhaust what we want to say. In Decree 4 it is justice **among men and women** that is involved: *Suum cuique tradere* (to render to each what is his due), in the words of the old and unequivocal definition. This applies to every kind of good which members of the human family can enjoy—material goods, to be sure, and also such immaterial goods as can be enjoyed on this earth. Examples of the latter are reputation, dignity, the possibility of exercising freedom.

Jesuits had no reason to be surprised that justice was under discussion and that they would hear more on the topic. In 1965 had not General Congregation 31 spoken about the social apostolate, which was declared to be "fully in harmony with the apostolic end of the Society"? It was that kind of justice which "strives directly by every endeavor to build a fuller expression of justice and charity into the structures of human life in common" (D. 32, no. 1).

Father John Baptist Janssens, the predecessor of Father Arrupe as superior general of the Society of Jesus, had defined the end of the social apostolate in these words:

> . . . to put within the reach of as many as possible, or even within the reach of all, the material and spiritual helps available, if not in plenty and abundance, at least in reasonable sufficiency. For that is what man needs to keep that self-confidence and self-respect which will enable him to rise superior to trials and temptations.[1]

In the same way, then, justice is described in Decree 4 of General Congregation 32, though its meaning is indeed extended to cover every Jesuit apostolate. More exactly, in this statement we read of justice and injustices, of material goods and resources. To speak this way about justice is very important for Christians; for there was indeed a time when questions of justice were all too little discussed, and strict obligations were passed over while attention was more turned towards charity, which was understood as generous and free, coming from the kind heart of the one concerned. But this "charity" risked being hypocritical.

### Justice Understood in a Very Broad Sense

Nonetheless, Decree 4, like the synod of bishops in 1971, does not speak only of justice in a very precise and narrow sense, which comes into play when there is question of clear obligations. It is to this sort of justice that the simple formula "To each his own" refers. Rather, it often speaks of justice in a wider sense, justice which comes into play when situations are encountered which are humanly intolerable and demand a remedy. Such situations can be the fruit

---

[1] J. B. Janssens, S.J. "Instruction on the Social Apostolate," *Acta Romana* 11, no. 5 (1949): 714.

of explicitly unjust acts perpetrated by clearly identified people, who, however, cannot be compelled to redress or to correct the wrong. Our humanity, however, requires that we find a remedy for this situation, if we wish to put it that way. But this is justice in the true sense of the word, for human dignity cannot otherwise be restored. There are other situations objectively unjust but for which those who are responsible cannot be identified. Certain kinds of inequality belong in this category. They cry, nonetheless, to heaven, once they are encountered. Injustices to be sure, if only in an objective sense.

The concern for justice found in Decree 4 includes all of these categories. So what is involved is not justice in some narrow, constrained, or restrictive sense. This comes out in references to injustices which are in part "structural." This we encounter in the following paragraph, for example:

> There is a new challenge to our apostolic mission in a world increasingly interdependent but, for all that, divided by injustice: injustice not only personal but institutionalized: built into economic, social, and political structures that dominate the life of nations and the international community. (no. 6 [52])

This understanding of justice clearly goes beyond relatively determined kinds of injustice.

This is true too in the following statement: "There are millions of men and women in our world, specific people with names and faces, who are suffering from poverty and hunger, from unjust distribution of wealth and resources . . ." (no. 20 [69]). It is not always, then, a matter of injustices for which a clear determination of responsibility is possible; but the situation is unjust, intolerable. This meaning is likewise found in the following lines: "Not only the quality of life but human life itself is under constant threat. It is becoming more and more clear that despite the opportunities offered by an ever more serviceable technology, we are simply not willing to pay the price of a more just and more humane society" (no. 20 [69]).

In such situations, then, it is not so much a question of identifying who is responsible as of underlining the responsibility which falls upon all those at least who become aware of the injustice and are able to bring a solution to it. (We can ask, it is true, whether excessive confidence is not placed here and there in "the opportunities offered by an ever more serviceable technology.")

Another phrase may perhaps seem to contradict our interpretation: "We can no longer pretend that the inequalities and injustices of our world must be borne as part of the inevitable order of things. It is now quite apparent that they are the result of what man himself, man in his selfishness, has done" (no. 27 [76]).

Now it is clear that with words like these the role of free will is brought into the picture. The point of the quotation, however, lies once again in the rejection above all of a fatalistic resignation, and in the affirmation of our own responsibility **today**. Furthermore, a few lines earlier we read: "It is now within human power to make the world more just—but we do not really want to." What is in question is our responsibility today rather than in the past.

> Our new mastery over nature and man himself is used, often enough, to exploit individuals, groups and peoples rather than to distribute the resources of the planet more equitably. It has led, it is leading, to division rather than union, to alienation rather than communication, to oppression and domination rather than to a greater respect for the rights of individuals or of groups, and a more real brotherhood among men. (no. 27 [76])

### *Justice in the Economic Order but Not in That Order Alone*

On the other hand, does not Decree 4 understand justice in a purely economic sense, though, to be sure, in terms of distribution and equality?

We have, indeed, just seen in several quotations an insistence on economic inequality and on poverty and hunger. Once again, it must be said that this is realistic. And how necessary! It is clear, though, that other aspects of injustice as well as of justice are likewise considered. For example, the references to the threats to "human life and its quality"; "racial and political discrimination" (no. 20 [69]); and lack of respect for "the rights of individuals or of groups" (no. 27 [76]).

With reason, despite all this, some may have wanted more explicit reference to certain of those rights as well as to offenses against truth, so common today. It is beyond doubt that Pope John

XXIII, for example, had in very timely fashion brought together truth, justice, solidarity (love), and freedom as the basis for a truly human social life.[2]

General Congregation 33 in 1983 called to the attention of Jesuits a number of important fields. For example, a frankly spiritual one is so described: "the spiritual hunger of so many, particularly the young, who search for meaning and values in a technological culture." On the other hand, an area in part spiritual, in part economic: "economic oppression and spiritual needs of the unemployed, of poor and landless peasants, and of workers" (D. 1, 45 [48]).

Other areas indicated refer to a vast range of injustices that go well beyond those of an economic nature, such as the following:

- attacks by governments on human rights through assassination, imprisonment, torture, the denial of religious freedom and political expression, all of which cause so many to suffer, some of them fellow Jesuits
- the sad plight of millions of refugees searching for a permanent home, a situation brought to our special attention by Father Arrupe
- discrimination against whole categories of human beings, such as migrants and racial or religious minorities
- the unjust treatment and exploitation of women
- public policies and social attitudes which threaten human life for the unborn, the handicapped and the aged. . . . (no. 45 [48])

If, then, one or other Jesuit could previously have entertained any doubts, it is very clear from this that the mission of the Society includes the widest possible view of justice. It includes very explicitly the preservation of international peace in the face of threats rising from recourse to nuclear arms.

We should note, moreover, that this listing comes close to that of the 1973 synod of bishops in its document "Justice in the World." Their list refers to victims of injustice deprived of the possibility of making themselves heard and understood. It is worth reproducing this document here even though it is quite lengthy:

---

[2] *Pacem in terris,* in *The Pope Speaks* 9, no. 1 (1963): nos. 81, 163.

Migrants are often forced to leave their own country to find work, but frequently find the doors closed in their faces because of discriminatory attitudes, or, if they can enter, they are often obliged to lead an insecure life or are treated in an inhuman manner. The same is true of groups that are less well off on the social ladder such as workers and especially farm workers who play a very great part in the process of development. To be especially lamented is the condition of so many millions of refugees, and of every group of people suffering persecution—sometimes in institutionalized form—for racial or ethnic origin or on tribal grounds. This persecution on tribal grounds can at times take on the characteristics of genocide. In many areas justice is seriously injured with regard to people who are suffering persecution for their faith, or who are in many ways being ceaselessly subjected by political parties and public authorities to an action of oppressive atheization, or who are deprived of religious liberty either by being kept from honoring God in public worship, or by being prevented from publicly teaching and spreading their faith, or by being prohibited from conducting their temporal affairs according to the principles of their religion.

Justice is also being violated by forms of oppression, both old and new, springing from restriction of the rights of individuals. This is occurring both in the form of repression by the political power and of violence on the part of private reaction, and can reach the extreme of affecting the basic conditions of personal integrity. There are well known cases of torture, especially of political prisoners, who besides are frequently denied due process or who are subjected to arbitrary procedures in their trial. Nor can we pass over the prisoners of war who even after the Geneva Convention are being treated in an inhuman manner.

The fight against legalized abortion and against the imposition of contraceptives as well as the pressures exerted against war are significant forms of defending the right to life.

Furthermore, contemporary consciousness demands truth in the communications systems, including the right to objectivity in the image offered by the media and the opportunity to correct its manipulation. It must be stressed that the right, especially that of children and the young, to education and to morally correct conditions of life and communications media is once again being threatened in our days. The activity of families in social life is rarely and insufficiently recognized by State institutions. Nor should we forget the growing number of persons who are often abandoned by their families and by the community; the old, orphans, the sick and all kinds of people who are rejected.[3]

## Far from Marxist Views

Even if Decree 4 was understood only literally, it was not fair to give the impression that its concept of justice was contaminated by a Marxist view of things. It is true that there is considerable insistence on social structures, but not necessarily in a Marxist sense. There can be no doubt, however, that the general congregation's document, with its insistence on human freedom, selfishness, and sin as underlying inequalities and injustices, was clearly far different from a Marxist view. After stressing the egoism and sin of humankind, it could say: "Hence there can be no promotion of justice in the full and Christian sense unless we also preach Jesus Christ and the mystery of reconciliation He brings." What is at stake is nothing less than liberation from sin, liberation "for which we long from the bottom of our hearts" (no. 27 [76]).

## Justice According to the Gospel

We see, then, that if Decree 4 directly concerns justice among people —human justice, not that by which God justifies the person in changing him from his previous state of sinfulness, as Paul explained justification—it is not so far from the justice of the Gospel. In fact, in its own words, it is the "perfect justice of the Gospel" which it explicitly invokes.

What is to be said? We find our answer in a very characteristic paragraph where the idea of justice is broad and quite free of any taint of merely commutative justice, free too of the spirit of simple insistence on one's own rights. This view of justice, on the contrary, implies nothing less than pardon, reconciliation, and mercy.

The Gospel demands a life freed from egoism and self-seeking, from all attempts to seek one's own advantage and from every form of exploitation of one's neighbor. It demands a life in which the justice of the Gospel shines out in a willingness not only to recognize and

---

[3] *Justice in the World,* 518f, nos. 21–26.

respect the rights of all, especially the poor and the powerless, but also to work actively to secure those rights. It demands an openness and generosity to anyone in need, even a stranger or an enemy. It demands toward those who have injured us, pardon; toward those with whom we are at odds, a spirit of reconciliation. (D. 4, no. 18 [67])

"The perfect justice of the Gospel." Such an expression is thoroughly justified. For "Gospel justice" refers to that attitude of respect for the smallest and weakest, attention to their rights and suffering, including those of an enemy. It goes all the way to pardon and reconciliation, as one finds it depicted on every page of the Gospel in both the example and teachings of Jesus. Justice nonetheless, for it clearly concerns giving to each one what is his due without causing the slightest wound, and in fact extending itself to the extreme limit of that which is required by human dignity. True justice, however, beyond what is often understood by that word. The great difference between this and the ordinary view of justice is that it is not so much concerned with making claims for one's own advantage as with carefully seeing to it that justice is done to others, and in particular to those who are the victims of injustice or in danger of becoming so—the little ones, the weak, the stranger, those without power.

### Relation to the Justice of God Who Justifies

Now, finally, we must explain the relation between justice as depicted above and the justice of God, of which St. Paul speaks. At first sight one would say that they are totally different and that there is no relationship between the two uses of the term. On the one hand, we have justice among people and on the other, justice in the relationship between the human person and God. On the one hand, justice is our work; on the other, it is the work of God himself, for God it is who "justifies" the sinner.

Now, despite all that, Decree 4 had to refer to the fifth chapter of Paul's Letter to the Romans, particularly to the following well-known lines: "But God demonstrates His own love towards us, in that while we were yet sinners, Christ died for us." "For one will hardly die for a righteous man," but Christ died for an unjust person, thus making him just (Rom 5:7–9).

What is the relation between that justice with which only God can grace the human person and the justice which the latter tries to assure to others? Decree 4 offers this explanation: Justice in its purity, the "perfect justice of the Gospel" which has just been described, is in its perfection beyond human possibility. We can approach it only if we are helped by the efficacious work of Christ himself, which makes just the sinner. "We do not acquire this attitude of mind by our own efforts alone. It is the fruit of the Spirit who transforms our hearts and fills them with the power of God's mercy, that mercy whereby he most fully shows forth His justice by drawing us, unjust though we are, to His friendship" (no. 18 [67]).

In the end, it is a matter of being just as God himself is just. God is the one who reconciles, indeed, who turns into just and lovable people those who were unjust. To this point we are called in our imitation of him even if we are still far off. Being thoroughly just means reaching out in pardon and reconciliation, the perfection of justice.

There is, then, a link between human justice, which Decree 4 addresses, and divine justice, thanks to which God makes just those who were unjust. Even when it speaks very openly about justice among people, Decree 4 does not present us with a goal which is simply of this world; it looks to the "perfect justice of the Gospel," as we have seen. Now we are in a position to add that it even looks to our human imitation of God himself and that unique justice through which he freely justifies the sinner.

# Chapter Six

# JUSTICE AND CHARITY

ustice thus perfects itself in love, even love of the most selfless
kind. Quite naturally, one might say. A real continuity appears
between justice, understood as total respect for the rights and
dignity of other persons, and a spirit of pardon and mercy, which
always looks to the person, but the person now considered beyond
his limitations, even indeed beyond his many acts of injustice and
his seeming or real unworthiness. So it is in discovering the link
between justice and charity that one begins to clarify just how justice is related to the faith.

## The Link Between Justice and Charity in Decree 4

In a later chapter we shall consider this question of the relation
between love of God and love of the human person. At the moment
our task is to insist on the existence of a link between the demands
of justice and love for the human person. First of all, we see that in
Decree 4 itself such a bond is, as a matter of fact, clearly present.
The statement to that effect in a key passage of the decree is really
and totally clear. "There is no genuine conversion to the love of God
without conversion to the love of neighbor and, **therefore,** to the
demands of justice" (no. 28 [77], emphasis added). The work of justice, then, is an integral part of love for our neighbor; it is demanded by that love.

Further, we can say that to love certainly has a wider application than to act justly, but the former without doubt requires the
latter. On the other hand, in Decree 4 no other **motive** for justice is
envisaged than fraternal love between person and person. Certainly,
in the ultimate analysis, that love in turn is founded on love for
God. Can we, moreover, base justice on anything other than love if

we truly desire to do justice and to be just—not simply seek our rights?

## *Remaining Questions*

The point, then, is beyond doubt in Decree 4, and the relation be-tween justice and love of neighbor is affirmed at a truly crucial point in the argument—not at all in passing or by chance. However, that affirmation is not developed in a very profound way. Some thought that it might go unnoticed. In any event, it is a fact that Father Arrupe soon began to be concerned about a particular view of the matter held by certain Jesuits; namely, an understanding of justice as something utterly inflexible and rigorous, as if actually separated from charity. It was, then, as if justice were sufficient in itself, perhaps more or less explicitly buttressed by an ideology which had no place for the Christian principle of love.

During the summer of 1980, therefore, Father Arrupe worked to prepare a text on charity and, in particular, on its relation to justice. We have already referred to that document. Further, he soon learned that Pope John Paul II was preparing an encyclical on mer-cy. That encyclical, *Dives in misericordia* (*Rich in Mercy*), appeared in autumn, and Father Arrupe used the occasion of the conclusion of a month-long seminar on Ignatian matters to present his thoughts in the closing conference on February 6, 1981.

We can say that the concerns of these two men ran along re-markably similar lines, an indication at the same time of a problem which would persist. So, in order to shed light on this matter, it will be worth the effort to gather together the essential thought of both authors.

## *Thoughts of Pope John Paul II*

In his encyclical the Pope first laid out at length the centrality of the mercy of God in Christian revelation, in both the Old and the New Testament, especially in the "paschal mystery" of the passion and death of Jesus Christ. On this point he writes:

> The cross on Calvary, the cross upon which Christ conducts his
> final dialogue with the Father, emerges from the very heart of the

love that man, created in the image and likeness of God, has been given as a gift, according to God's eternal plan. God, as Christ has revealed him, does not merely remain closely linked with the world as the creator and the ultimate source of existence. He is also Father: He is linked to man, whom he called to existence in the visible world, by a bond still more intimate than that of creation. It is love which not only creates the good but also grants participation in the very life of God: Father, Son and Holy Spirit. For he who loves desires to give himself.[1]

He then adds:

The cross of Christ on Calvary stands on the path of that *admirabile commercium,* of that wonderful self-communication of God to man, which also includes the call to man to share in the divine life by giving himself, and with himself the whole visible world, to God, and like an adopted son to become a sharer in the truth and love which is in God and proceeds from God. (no. 7)

Basing his thought on this consideration of the love of a merciful God which we too are called to share, Pope John Paul II regards today's world with all the sources of disquiet encountered there, starting with the threat of nuclear self-destruction. He then depicts the abuses of power to which some subject others; types of "peaceful" subjugation on the part of individuals, whole societies and nations; famine, inequalities, materialism. He points out how in response to this ugly reality

[i]t is not difficult to see that in the modern world the sense of justice has been reawakening on a vast scale. . . . This deep and varied trend, at the basis of which the contemporary human conscience has placed justice, gives proof of the ethical character of the tensions and struggles pervading the world. (no. 12)

He then makes clear how the Church "shares with the people of our time this profound and ardent desire which is just in every aspect," but then asks, "Is justice enough?" He responds with these serious and important reflections, very much to the point:

And yet it would be difficult not to notice that very often programs which start from the idea of justice and which ought to assist its fulfillment among individuals, groups and human societies, in practice suffer from distortions. Although they continue to

---

[1] *Dives in misericordia,* in *Origins* 10, no. 26 (Dec. 11, 1980): no. 7.

appeal to the ideal of justice, nevertheless experience shows that other negative forces have gained the upper hand over justice, such as spite, hatred and even cruelty.

In such cases, the desire to annihilate the enemy, limit his freedom or even force him into total dependence, becomes the fundamental motive for action; and this contrasts with the essence of justice, which by its nature tends to establish equality and harmony between the parties in conflict. This kind of abuse of the idea of justice and the practical distortion of it show how far human action can deviate from justice itself, even when it is being undertaken in the name of justice. (no. 12)

With even greater precision the Pope remarks: "It is obvious, in fact, that in the name of an alleged justice (for example, historical justice or class justice) the neighbor is sometimes destroyed, killed, deprived of liberty or stripped of fundamental human rights" (no. 12).

Is the misuse of justice, then, a necessary element in the search for justice? Is it preordained that justice is so deflected from its ideal? The Pope in truth does not answer these questions, but he observes:

The experience of the past and of our own time demonstrates that justice alone is not enough, that it can even lead to the negation and destruction of itself, if that deeper power, which is love, is not allowed to shape human life in its various dimensions.

It has been precisely historical experience that, among other things, has led to the formulation of the saying: *Summum ius, summa iniuria* (Justice taken to the extreme leads to extreme injustice). This statement does not detract from the value of justice and does not minimize the significance of the order that is based upon it; it only indicates, under another aspect, the need to draw from the powers of the spirit which condition the very order of justice, powers which are still more profound. (no. 12)

The Pope then vigorously underlines how justice alone is not enough. He also shows—briefly, to be sure—the link between justice and love and one might say, the inclusion of the former in the latter. "Love, so to speak, conditions justice and, in the final analysis, justice serves love" (no. 12).

As was previously observed, this is the meaning of the words of Decree 4: "conversion to the love of neighbor and, **therefore**, to the demands of justice" (no. 28 [77], emphasis added).

## The Thought of Father Arrupe

In *Rich in Mercy* we find the phrase just referred to, love being a condition for justice and justice being in the service of love. This phrase Father Arrupe used in his 1981 conference *Rooted and Grounded in Love.*

He also quoted the following from the 1971 synod of bishops: "Love of neighbor and justice are inseparable. Love is above all a requirement of justice, that is, an acknowledgment of the dignity and of the rights of one's neighbor."[2] So justice first of all, if one wishes to love. On the other hand, if there is no sense of love and if one does not love, one must fear that even the quest for justice will become degraded. His words were, "Even when we resist injustice we cannot prescind from love, since the universality of love is, by the express desire of Christ, a commandment that admits of no exceptions" (no. 56).

Again, a little earlier he says:

When a God-given right is disregarded or repressed by a "legal" injustice, it provokes the reaction of an illegal "justice." Not every legal justice is objectively just. To reduce the distance that separates justice from law is one of the prime objectives of any social and authentically human progress. But that can never be achieved as long as law and justice are not infused with charity. (no. 55)

Clearly, Father Arrupe showed that he was aware of the abuse which could come equally from the side of love, "false love." He wrote:

There is an apparent charity, though, that is a mere cloak for injustice, when people are given, apart from the law and as if by benevolence, what is their due in justice. It is almsgiving as a subterfuge. Tyrannical regimes that impose laws violating rights, and paternalistic systems that offer "charitable" aid programs instead of a clear policy of justice, are evils that make impossible the establishment of brotherhood and peace among men. (no. 56)

It is no less important to underline how justice is included in love, thought Father Arrupe. And love is always first.

---

[2] *Rooted and Grounded in Love,* in *Documentation,* no. 47 (Rome: Press and Information Office of the Society of Jesus, 1981), no. 56.

He went on to present his view that justice is insufficient, even when it is neither betrayed nor altered.

> Obviously, the promotion of justice is indispensable, because it is the first step to charity. To claim justice sometimes seems revolutionary, a subversive claim. And yet, it is so small a request: we really ought to ask for more, we should go beyond justice, to crown it with charity. Justice is necessary, but it is not enough. Charity adds its transcendent, inner dimension to justice and, when it has reached the limits of the realm of justice, can keep going even further. Because justice has its limits, and stops where rights terminate; but love has no boundaries because it reproduces, on our human scale, the infiniteness of the divine essence and gives to each of our human brothers a claim to our unlimited service. (no. 57)

Another statement in the same vein follows shortly after. "Love for one's neighbor gives not only this or that—as justice does—but one's whole self . . ." (no. 59).

As a matter of fact, however, love does not only go beyond justice but "gives it a hand." It aids justice as it moves forward in pursuit of the new demands laid upon it. Neither is justice as far behind as at first it appears.

> And we may add that our knowledge of the extent of human rights is far from being complete. Just as we still do not know the limit of man's physical capacities, as seemingly unbeatable records keep falling, so we cannot determine what a thoroughly developed moral conscience and a sense of Christian brotherhood and equality will some day affirm to be the full scope of human rights. (no. 60)

Moreover, a clear understanding of the demands of justice is not enough for those demands to be realized; once again, charity is essential if they are to be realized.

> But does not our increasingly clear knowledge of what are the rights to which justice is correlative, when contrasted with the extremely bitter reality we see around us, reveal a disillusioning contradiction between our hopes and that reality? Only charity can, by seeing to it that justice is applied in all its amplitude, keep injustice from erupting in the tragic violence that we must constantly deplore. (no. 60)

Such statements lead us right back to the concern which Pope John Paul II expressed: the difference between the will for justice and injustice committed in the name of justice; the need, therefore, for love as a remedy for this lack as well as for this distortion of justice.

Father Arrupe then quotes the Pope (*Summum ius, summa iniuria*) and adds the following reflections of his own:

> There are versions of justice that take no account of the concrete existential situation of the persons and conditions to which it is applied. There are kinds of justice that are a cover-up for vested interests. A justice, a law that demands too little, leaves the helpless or oppressed man defenceless. So too, a violent law, a violent justice that demands too much, can become a hangman's noose for everyone. And even a justice with all the guarantees of equity can, if mercilessly applied, be inhuman. (no. 61)

It is often necessary, then, for us, "urged by charity, to go beyond the law." " This is the charity that among men must complement justice, making it a higher sort of justice. It is the only one that can go on, beyond mere justice, to the point of meeting the needs of men" (no. 61).

Now, what is this "superior form of justice" just referred to? It is, says Father Arrupe, "a justice which sees everything with a more penetrating scope too, since it plunges down to the inmost depths of man, to his pain, his need, his helplessness, which are realities that are lost sight of when he is treated impersonally, as a mere subject of the law" (no. 62).

Towards the end of his conference, he returns to the same theme, crying out:

> Yes, justice is not enough. The world needs a stronger cure, a more effective witness and more effective deeds: those of love. When we glance over the newspaper headlines and seek somehow for the real reason why human relations are at such a low ebb— within the family, the state, the world of work, the economic order, and internationally—every explanation in terms of justice and injustice seems inadequate. Never have people talked so much about justice, and yet never has justice been so flagrantly disregarded. (no. 68)

And sketching a dark picture of evil, of that "anomie" which, according to St. Matthew (24:12) goes on growing, Father Arrupe says:

> The right of might replaces the might of right: it nullifies God's command, revealed in Jesus, that love and brotherhood should rule

the relationships among men. It is, in the technical sense, the rule of immorality, ethical degeneration. Anomía is the absence of justice, iniquity in its etymological sense: the absence of equity, injustice. (no. 69)

Salvation comes only through love (agape), which St. Matthew contrasts with anomie. Father Arrupe continued:

> Agapé: a disinterested impulse that leads us to understand, to empathize, to share, to help and to heal, born of faith in the love that God has for us and that we see revealed in our brothers. That love is still being given in today's world. As Nadal used to say, it is a flame that has always been lit, and still is, in the Church and in our least Society, and that we strive to keep alive and quicken. . . . Agapé is the evangelical message of love and of peace, all that gives meaning to the life that is born of faith, both personal and communitarian or social. (no. 71)

### The Final Step Beyond the Choice for the Promotion of Justice

In this conference Father Arrupe did not intend to add anything to Decree 4; instead, he deliberately strove to call attention to some of its aspects which at times were overlooked; in particular, the essential link between "justice" and "love for neighbor," in short, charity (D. 4, no. 28 [77]).

Taking up again the thread of events since General Congregation 32 and Decree 4, which had situated the promotion of justice at the very heart of Jesuit mission, along with service of the faith, he wrote:

> That decision seemed a great step forward, and the Society has been striving since then to carry it out. We still need perspective to evaluate the current balance of well-meant failures and undeniable successes which that option has produced in the Church through the Society. In the light of the most recent encyclical, *Dives in misericordia*, we may say that, with all the imperfections of any human choice, it was an option in the right direction. However, this is not sufficient, it is not the last step. The Congregation realized that charity is the "final step" and basis of everything, and that true justice starts from and is crowned in charity. (*Rooted and Grounded*, no. 67)

He looked again at the statements in Decree 4 touching on the link between justice and charity and between justice and the spirit of the Beatitudes. He concluded his reflections with the following words:

> We should keep these paragraphs of Decree 4 well in mind, so that our reading of it will not be incomplete, slanted and unbalanced. The Society still has to advance in its understanding of, and search for, that justice which it has pledged itself to promote. I am sure that effort will lead us to discover an even wider field—that of charity. (no. 67)

The same understanding of justice and of its relation to charity is later found in the decree formulated by General Congregation 33 to deal with the mission of the Society. In relation to the past, we have already seen the words in question. "We have not always recognized that the social justice we are called to is part of that justice of the Gospel which is the embodiment of God's love and saving mercy" (D. 1, 32 [35]). Justice as the embodiment of the very love and mercy of God is indeed a new notion, very much in line, it is true, with all the descriptions of justice as an integrating part of charity.

In what concerns the future, the hope is that by means of a profound and renewed strengthening of religious and community life, Jesuits would make themselves able to "understand better how the service of the faith and the promotion of justice are not two juxtaposed, much less conflicting, goals but a single commitment which finds its coherence and deepest expression in that love of God and love of neighbor to which God calls us in the One Great Commandment" (no. 42 [45]). In this context some of the words which we have just seen are incorporated from Father Arrupe's conference: "One cannot act justly without love. Even when we resist unjustice, we cannot prescind from love, since the universality of love is, by the express desire of Christ, a commandment that admits of no exception" (*Rooted and Grounded*, no. 56).

### Justice Integrated with Charity Always Envisaged

The statements of Decree 4 on the link between justice and charity were always clear, but they had not been developed so thoroughly.

Today, in response to the question on the nature of justice as found in Decree 4, we can reply with even greater assurance that it presents justice as rooted in charity, its supreme motivation; further, that it is in this way an integrating part of charity, which in turn is always able to lead us to discover new demands of justice, which is not something fixed once and for all; finally, that even while satisfying the claims of justice, we must never violate charity, which always extends beyond the bounds of justice.

In the previous chapter we have already commented on the strict relation between justice and Gospel teaching, if indeed there is a "perfect justice" of the Gospel, learned through the example and teachings of Christ; learned also from the example of God himself, who through his Son's passion and death turns sinful humans into just persons meeting his approval, unable though they were to lessen the distance between God and themselves. In this chapter we have underlined even more strongly that, thanks to Decree 4, justice is seen to be linked with, regulated, and almost enveloped by love of neighbor. This we were able to see, thanks also to the reflections of Pope John Paul II in his encyclical *Dives in misericordia* and to Father Arrupe's conference *Rooted and Grounded in Love.*

Further, through this allusion to the link between unity of the commandment of love of God and love of neighbor, we have begun to open ourselves to a perspective where justice—only as it draws near to love—draws near to faith too, in accordance with the very title of Decree 4.

# Chapter Seven

## LOVE OF GOD AND LOVE OF NEIGHBOR

T he relation of faith to charity and of faith to justice, which the former demands and inspires, is not adequately understood unless there is a close relation between love of God and love of neighbor. As we shall see, Decree 4 very clearly and forcefully leads us back to that relation of love of God and love of neighbor; in the response of the human person to God's call, the love of God is inseparable from the love of the human person. This teaching is fully traditional. At the same time, however, we are invited to carry our study to a deeper level, as some Jesuit theologians did under the stimulation of Decree 4. They tried to show that the love of God is also implied in human love. So the relation of the two loves thus becomes very explicit and their deep unity comes to be better understood. We will seek now to make their view our own.

### *In Decree 4*

In Decree 4, no. 28 [77], which is central to its argument, we read the explanation that, in accord with Christian teaching, all of us are called to be converted and that this conversion has two aspects indissolubly linked: "Christian salvation consists in an undivided love of the Father and of the neighbor and of justice." Love of God and love of neighbor. The point of this text becomes even clearer in the following phrase: "There is no genuine conversion to the love of God without conversion to the love of neighbor."

This does not mean, of course, that human love is a preamble to love of God; rather, it is to accompany that love. The call to conversion, then, is a call to the love of God but not as independent from the other love, that of the neighbor. The text we are considering ends as follows: "Christian salvation consists in an undivided love of the Father and of the neighbor and of justice. Since evangelization is proclamation of that faith which is made operative in love of others [Gal. 5:6, Eph. 4:15], the promotion of justice is indispensable to it (no. 28 [77]).

Why, we may ask, are these two obligations—love of God and love of neighbor—inseparable? We find no lengthy explanation in the decree itself; nevertheless, the following words are tantamount to an explanation: "At the heart of the Christian message is God revealing Himself in Christ as the Father of us all" (no. 28 [77]). Since God is "Father" of each of us, we all owe him a loving response, which is the "attitude of children to Him"; in other words, the love of God. Since God is Father "of all men and women," we are all, then, his children; and nobody can truly love God unless that love also embraces all mankind, his brothers and sisters.

### Consideration in Depth

As we indicated, some Jesuits have subsequently attempted to develop this basic explanation further. This was the case in Germany, for instance, where Walter Kerber, Karl Rahner, and Hans Zwiefelhofer were asked after General Congregation 32 to make a deeper study of the relation between the service of the faith and the promotion of justice. At the beginning of 1976, they wrote on this subject as follows:

> What is the theological locus in which this problem is really addressed and where does it fit into the the Church's traditional teaching? It seems to us that probably the most relevant theological locus is where there has been reflection, on the basis of the sources of revelation and through the mediation of theology, upon the simultaneous **unity and difference obtaining between love of God and love of neighbor.**[1]

In their view, then, the need was not so much to make explicit the link between justice and charity—a link that is rather obvious once charity is no longer considered as limited to an exclusively private domain of existence, and justice is given its full social

---

[1] [Translator's note: This and the following quotations are taken from unpublished material available to the author.]

dimension and its dimension of social criticism—nor to make explicit the link between faith and charity as love of God, since this love embraces the totality of one's relation to God, including, therefore, faith (*fides caritate formata*). The crucial issue was, rather, that of the relation between love of God and love of neighbor. Our authors examine this at length.

They look at the New Testament. First, the Gospel. The Second Commandment is similar to the First; on the last day a person is judged on his love for the neighbor; the cooling of this love is the "iniquity" which is a harbinger of the end of time; what is done to the least of human beings is done to Jesus. Then they turn to St. Paul. Love for the neighbor is presented as the fulfillment of the law, the bond of perfection, the most excellent way—in brief, the summation of the form of Christian existence. Finally, they refer to St. John. We are loved by God **so that** we may love each other, this love being the new commandment of Christ; or, again, God has loved us, not so much or not explicitly so that we might love him in return, but so that we might love each other. All this, our authors tell us, does not yet permit us to draw very precise conclusions; at the least, "the overall relation to God" is remarkably "centered on fraternal love."

Traditional theology, they point out, considers authentic Christian charity—genuine love of neighbor—"an integral part of the infused and supernatural virtue of *caritas,* by which we love God in his Spirit and for his own sake, in an immediate nearness to him." In this perspective, love of neighbor is not simply a preliminary "condition, effect, and touchstone of love for God," but is itself an "act of this love of God." At the very least, it is an act comprised in "that total abandonment of self to God by faith and love which we call love of God," by which a person is justified, reconciled, reunited to God.

Resorting, then, to Rahner's "transcendental" conception, our authors give this explanation: Not every act of love for God is formally an act of love of neighbor; but conversely, "wherever the full transcendental depth of interhuman love is present (a love which at least **can** be *caritas* according to the best tradition), this love is also necessarily, by that very fact, love of God; it has God as its reflexive motive (although, of course, with greater or lesser degrees of clarity)." This is the first point.

On the other hand, continue the three German Jesuits, we cannot say that every act of love of neighbor is at the same time explicitly an act of love of God. Rather, the act of love of neighbor has the love of God as its "transcendental horizon." Thus, of itself the act of love of neighbor is oriented towards God, albeit not in an explicit way (*unthematisch*). Every positive moral act, they also comment, possesses in a hidden and "anonymous" way a Christian character (*anonyme Christlichkeit jedes positiv sittlichen Tuns*).

Finally, if all this is true, given that human beings cannot directly apprehend God himself, whereas they constantly exist surrounded by their human brothers and sisters, we can say that it is through love for the neighbor that love for God becomes visible.

> One's basic relation to God is transcendental in character; it does not belong to the world of objects. It appears in that unlimited openness (*unendliche Verwiesenheit*) beyond the objects of the environment which characterizes the human spirit. Consequently, the primordial experience of God (*ursprüngliche Erfahrung Gottes*)—as opposed to the isolated representation of it in a particular concept— does not present itself apart from an experience of the world (*weltiche Erfahrung*). The latter, however, in its primordial and total meaning, is present only in communication with the Thou.

Thus, there is a profound unity between love of the neighbor and love of God, in the sense that love of neighbor, *caritas*, "is not merely a dependent moral act among many similar such acts 'decreed' by *caritas*, understood as love for God." Love of neighbor is, on the contrary, already love for God; or, it is a love which, within the relation of charity towards the neighbor, aims always at God himself—in itself, indeed, or by supernatural transcendentality, but still in a very real manner. The relation of love of neighbor to love of God is not merely that of a moral or psychological exigency, but also that of a "radical" or ontological implication. This is the full explanation, in our authors' view, of the text "Whoever does not love his brother, whom he sees, cannot love God, whom he does not see" (1 John 4:20).

We should point out that, while this thesis shows how love of God is always already implicit in love of neighbor, it in no way sets aside the obligation to love God in an entirely explicit fashion. On the contrary, there is no full and integral love of neighbor without an express gratitude and love towards God grounding our love for the neighbor. "Love of the neighbor is not fully achieved until it reaches its ultimate foundation, its definitive guarantee, by means of an express awareness of this foundation which is God and by means of an equally explicit relation to him." Love of the neighbor thus transcends and sublimates itself (*wird aufgehoben*) in explicit love of God, which as such is higher than love for the neighbor taken in its merely empirical content.

Thus, there is no question of reducing one of the two terms, one of the two loves, to the other—just as one cannot reduce to each other experience of the world and experience of God. But the unity of the two loves is truly strong, "ontological." It goes beyond implying that the love of God morally requires the love of the neighbor.

### Father Arrupe's Views on the Unity of the Two Loves

In simpler terms than those used in the analysis of transcendental theology, Father Arrupe's 1981 conference *Rooted and Grounded in Love* offered an explanation of the same unity of the two loves in the context of the conviction of a **unique** underlying love: "God is love" ("the very last root, the ultimate foundation of the Ignatian charism, the soul of the Society" [no. 1]).

He developed his explanation as follows:

> As far as one can deal with these matters in human terms, one could say that love at its purest—love in itself—is, on the one hand, the formal constitutive element of the divine essence and, on the other, the explanation and cause of the operations *ad extra:* the creation of man, lord of the universe, and the return of all things to God in a history of redemption and sanctification. This double formal aspect of love finds in Ignatius the echo of a double response; a sublime theocentric love, that is compatible with a marked presence of Christ even as man; and a boundless love of charity for his fellow men in whom God's love, as he sees it, is patently present, and who must be led back to God. (no. 2)

Referring to the autobiography of St. Ignatius, Father Arrupe said, "Ignatius succeeded in perfectly unifying his love of God, a most intense love directed totally to loving the Most Holy Trinity, with love for his fellowmen"[2] (no. 45).

He then spoke of that "integration of charity" which was lived and proclaimed by both St. Paul and St. John. First, St. Paul's love for Christ contains an apostolic thrust; and thus the best way Paul knows to satisfy his thirst for identification with Christ is by devoting himself to the service of men, concretely, of the "gentiles." This service is owed to all men, inasmuch as in every man, notably in the weaker ones, there is a brother for whom Christ died (no. 45, citing 1 Cor. 8:11).

In St. John, Father Arrupe stressed, the two loves are inseparably joined.

> To love our brothers, and to show this love in our actions, is not something adventitious, something added to our love of God to complete it. It is a constitutive element demanded by the very notion of the love of God. But we must make the converse statement too: by the very fact that we are Christians, we cannot genuinely love men unless we love God. (no. 48f)

The last point is then developed with originality in this manner:

> What is asked of us is not a love of "philanthropy," but a "philadelphia," a love of brotherhood. In every man, with all his concrete circumstances, there is a value that does not depend on me, but that makes him like me. God is within him, with his love, waiting for me, and this is a call that I cannot neglect. (no. 49).

So we see how Decree 4 has really led our attention back to the link between love of God and love of neighbor. In other words, we see how the views found in Decree 4 on the integration of service of the faith and the promotion of justice are based on the unity of those two loves. This is true, even if this theme is not developed at length in Decree 4 itself.

After eight years of deepening these reflections, some of the more meaningful of which we have just now seen, General Congregation 33 expressed its own conviction, as we have noted, that the service of the faith and the promotion of justice make up that "single commitment which finds its coherence and deepest expres-

---

[2] The emphasized words are taken from a letter of St. Ignatius to Jaime Cassador dated February 12, 1536.

sion in that love of God and love of neighbor to which God calls us in the One Great Commandment" (D. 1, no. 42 [45]). A note at this point calls our attention to five important Scriptural references: John 15:9–16, 1 John 4:7–20; Matt. 22:34–40; Mark 12:28–34; Luke 10:25–37. Equivalently we are thus offered a view on the basic importance of an attitude without which the relation of justice to faith and commitment to justice in service of the faith would remain distant indeed. Now we must still explain the relation of faith itself to charity, understood as love of God and love of neighbor. This we will now proceed to do.

# Chapter Eight

# FAITH AND CHARITY

Faith and charity have traditionally been called theological virtues. Along with hope, they form the trio of our major movements toward God himself. At the same time the relationship between the two—faith and charity—is not always clear to everyone, even when the unity of love of God and love of neighbor has been previously highlighted. It is appropriate, then, that we consider how Decree 4 and the reflections that followed its publication treat this question.

It is worthwhile to see if a more direct and immediate relation of faith and justice can be established without the express mediation of the faith—charity and the justice—charity relations. As we will see at the end of this chapter, such an effort has been made, and we will explore the interesting aspects, as well as the limitations of this question.

## Faith and Works

In the first place, it should be noted, we can never escape the problem of the relation between faith and good works, much discussed from apostolic times, as the writings of SS. Paul, James, and Peter testify. Even love for God, it seems to many, finds itself linked with works; although these are undoubtedly commanded by faith, they are not on the same level with it.

Simply and clearly Decree 4 affirms that "evangelization is proclamation of that faith which is made operative in love of others" (no. 28 [77]). Two references to St. Paul are adduced in support of this statement. "In Christ Jesus neither circumcision nor the lack of it counts for anything; only **faith, which expresses itself through love** (Gal. 5:6, emphasis added). In sum, faith and love are linked.

On the other hand, "Let us profess the truth in love and grow to the full maturity of Christ the head" (Eph. 4:15). For St. Paul, then, without love there is neither witness to the truth nor profession of faith.

In the same spirit, moreover, Decree 4 refers to attitudes which are contrary to justice as being equivalent to a lack of faith, that is, "atheism." Without works, where can faith be found? "The injustice that racks our world is, in fact, a denial of God in practice, for it denies the dignity of the human person, the image of God, the brother or sister of Christ" (no. 29 [78]).

### Father Arrupe's View

Father Arrupe had occasion to take up and develop these points, especially in his conference *Rooted and Grounded in Love.*

> Faith gives meaning to our charity, while charity activates and animates our faith. When Christ stimulates our faith in him and in the Father so that we will "know," he is asking of us not merely a witness—statement or an acknowledgement, but an acceptance of his identity as the One Sent and as the Son, an acceptance of his message of conversion; he is asking us to keep his commandments, especially the new commandment, his own commandment. (no. 50)

He then added, "Ignatius's 'interior knowledge' is no different from the 'faith,' the 'believing,' the 'knowing' that John speaks of; and it leads inexorably to action and to service, as it does in John" (no. 50).

A bit further on, in his comments on St. John, he offers this observation:

> For John, believing means knowing; it means entering into Christ and sharing in his life, his action and his message. At the same time it means letting oneself be penetrated by Christ. Thus faith, according to John, necessarily calls for love and the works of love, the work of charity. (no. 51)

St. James, Father Arrupe adds, teaches the same doctrine.

Father Arrupe then explains that, according to all three—SS. John, Paul, and James—

> if faith without works is not real faith, the converse is also true: charity without faith is not charity either. For Paul this is incon-

testable. His entire argumentation against Israel is based precisely on the insufficiency of works founded on the law, now that the hour of faith has come. What gives them value is faith. (no. 53)

He then cites St. Paul: "The pagans who were not looking for righteousness that comes of faith have obtained it, while Israel, looking for a righteousness derived from law, has not attained it. Why did they fail? Because they relied on good deeds instead of trusting in faith" (Rom. 9:30–32). Father Arrupe continues:

This Pauline criterion and analysis are still profoundly applicable today. I know very well that in this text Paul is referring to justification. But it still has all its value inasmuch as it condemns a salvation that we human beings strive to obtain—and to impose on others—on the basis of works, the assertion of rights and the imposition of obligations. We forget that it is faith that justifies, that makes us free, that blossoms into charity and gives meaning to our works. Faith without works is a dead faith. But works without faith, and without charity vitalizing it, are no more than well-meaning humanitarianism, philanthropy. (no. 54)

Along the same line, focusing on justice rather than explicitly on charity—though these are tightly linked, of course—Decree 4 affirms both the one and the other truth: "It will not be possible to bring Christ to people or to proclaim his Gospel effectively unless a firm decision is taken to devote ourselves to the promotion of justice" (no. 27 [76]). Faith without works, we have just said, is a dead faith. On the other hand, we read: "Hence there can be no promotion of justice in the full and Christian sense unless we also preach Jesus Christ and the mystery of reconciliation He brings. It is Christ who, in the last analysis, opens the way to the complete and definitive liberation of mankind for which we long from the bottom of our hearts" (no. 27 [76]). In what refers to salvation in the fullest sense and to "the complete and definitive liberation" towards which the human person tends, works without faith never suffice.

### An Even-closer Connection

As long as we speak in this way about faith and works, we are led to affirm very simply: neither faith without works nor works without faith suffice. But we can still remain without an intrinsic connection between the love of God and the love of neighbor, which we saw achieved in the preceding chapter. Now the question: Is there an equally profound connection between faith and charity, understood as love for God and the human person, but first and foremost for God?

The answer is that there is; faith and charity are connected very closely. In one sense, indeed, there is no true priority of the one over the other. On the other hand, however, the word "faith" refers to the access to the other, while "charity" refers to the union between the two. So, a difference is maintained between the two, and this difference is reflected in the relation between the service of the faith and the promotion of justice.

Often there is a tendency to place faith exclusively on the side of knowledge. Then, according to the person's natural inclination, one of two things happens: Either the individual sets little importance on faith and the service of the faith—a concern rather intellectual (after all, they say, we will be judged by another criterion!)—or, on the contrary, one is concerned almost exclusively with faith (for how can we love what we do not know?). Those of the second tendency do indeed see love connected with faith but as "commanded" by it; faith would command love as something apart from itself.

Knowledge and love are not so distinguished when we speak of God and the things of God, but they are so when the human world alone is under discussion. Even St. Thomas, who today is accused of being an intellectualist, understood faith in a very different sense. For him, "to believe" pertains to the intellect, but "as it is moved to assent by the will."[1] Again, he uses the expression "influenced by the will." Love is the "form" of faith, form understood as "the end to which the act is directed" (q. 4., art. 3). Faith, then, is truly included in love, which has primacy, not priority. Love, St. Thomas says, "attains God Himself to rest in Him"; faith and hope "certainly attain God, but insofar as through them knowledge of the truth and the possession of good" come to us (q. 23, art. 6).

A commentator on these expressions of Saint Thomas has said, "Considered from the viewpoint of origin, love is the third of the

---

[1] *Summa theologica,* vol. 31 (New York: McGraw-Hill Book Company, Blackfriars, 1974), 2a–2æ, q. 2, a. 2.

theological virtues, but in the order of excellence and of influence it is the first; for it becomes the vital principle and supreme motive for the supernatural conscience."[2] In the same spirit, Father Arrupe loved to say that charity is the principle both of faith and of justice.

In another context, Cardinal de Lubac, in the introduction to his commentary on the Creed, wrote as follows: "Faith is not only a mode of knowing. It is entirely different from a simple conviction. It is an essentially personal act, which, if correctly understood, involves the very core of our being, and entirely orientates it."[3] On the other hand, he goes on,

> When I believe in God and give him my faith, when in response to his initiative, I entrust myself to him from the core of my being, he sets up between himself and myself such a bond of reciprocity that the very word "faith" can refer to each of the partners; the "faith of both partners." St. John of the Cross with some daring describes the relationship of the believing soul with God. (145)

One senses in these lines the relation to charity, God by one and the same initiative loving and calling for the love that the other can return to him.

Of course, further on Cardinal de Lubac does not fail to insist on the relation between this basic entrusting of oneself to God and the acceptance of the objects of faith: it is as if faith in God is inevitably refracted in what is believed.

> The entire Christian tradition, clearly attested to from its very first days, unites *I believe in* and *I believe that* in a single act. It is in response to the gift which God gives us in His works (creation, redemption, sanctification) that we give ourselves to God in return. So as not to remain empty and formal, faith nourishes itself on belief, which it supposes, integrates, and encompasses. . . . Our faith is an adhesion to this word of God which fragments itself by objectifying itself in order to speak its message, be understood by us, and reach us in our terrestrial condition; only so do we rejoin it in its unity. (148)

---

[2] H. D. Noble, "Introduction," *La charité* (Éditions de la *Revue des Jeunes,* 1969) 1:6.

[3] Henri de Lubac, *La foi chrétienne* (Aubier, 1969), 144.

### A Certain Priority of Faith on the Psychological Plane

This clearly forbids us to think that our acceptance of the objects of faith—*I believe that*—is of little importance, as occasionally it has seemed that this or that theologian has done, because he was deeply concerned to see Christianity realized in charity, justice, and liberation. There is something still more fundamental; even if faith—*I believe in*—understood as the entrusting of self to God, is not given without love, even if love is the "form" of faith, there is a difference between the two, though only in our psychology, in our earthly approach to things. "Belief," says St. Thomas, "is immediately an act of the intellect, because its object is truth, which is the proper concern of intellect" (*Summa Theologica,* 2a–2æ, q. 4. a. 2). Now this difference entails a certain psychological priority of faith: we first give our trust to God, entrust ourselves to him, cleave to him in response to his gifts, before giving ourselves **in return**—to God and to other persons, our brothers and sisters—even if our act of entrusting ourselves to God is already the beginning of the gift of self. From this point of view, it is faith first of all that refracts itself in charity —love of God and neighbor—and goes on to include all that might be undertaken in order to make justice live.

Faith understood correctly, and not as a simple—and vain—intellectual exercise, appears, then, as central and essential in the efforts through which the person forms himself. It will be more or less able to express itself and to translate itself in different acts of belief, especially in those pertaining to the Church. In many, faith will perhaps remain implicit, but it is surely fundamental to the uniting of freedom with the absolute which gives life to it, to the transcendence of self toward one's brothers and sisters—an act which otherwise cannot be fully justified.

### But It Is Also Necessary Always to Return to Unity

It is in virtue of this priority that faith is listed first among the three theological virtues—faith, hope, and charity. It is also in virtue of the same priority that, at the very time that it was underlining the importance of the promotion of justice, the Society of Jesus described its own fundamental task by means of the expression "service of the faith"—assisting one's brothers and sisters to give themselves to God, to believe—as a description of its own fundamental task. Now we have also just seen the profound unity that exists between the movement of faith and that of charity. Just as there is no less unity between love for God and love for our fellows, we likewise see better how faith in its most theological sense summons us to love our brothers and sisters. Let us even say "demands" it, and thus approach the wording of Decree 4, which, as we have seen, speaks of the promotion of justice as an absolute demand of the service of the faith, and supposes that justice and the charity which includes it are likewise demanded by faith.

Let us underline how we have gone beyond the view that faith demands or commands the work of charity as a simple moral obligation, something external to the theological act, in particular, to the act of faith. The connection between the two truly appears much closer and more interior; faith is already seen as a movement towards the other, as a movement from the very depths of the being. Love itself is in no way equivalent to possession, not even of its own works; it means entrusting oneself, abandoning oneself, placing one's faith, in the last analysis, in God himself (when one gives it without reserve to one's brothers or sisters).

We have to use a terminology here which may seem to sound like the language of secularization, insofar as it gives so much importance to charity, understood as translating, expressing, animating faith. Actually, it sounds more like thoroughly religious language, because it gives so much value to faith, seen as ceaselessly leading charity back to its origin, to total abandonment. This is the context of Decree 4, these its theological foundations. These are truths which are thoroughly fundamental even though they may not often be in the limelight.

What is simple is not for that reason always evident, so it deserves to be deepened and reflected upon, especially when it involves very important considerations guiding the Christian conscience toward a just equilibrium in today's world. Conscience has often been tossed about in the post-conciliar period, left uncertain about the place of faith and charity and the relation between the two. Now, on the contrary, it seems that we can reach a peaceful alignment of the two without sacrificing either. In satisfying this condition, we can say that the most fundamental theological foundations of Decree 4 appear to be completely firm.

## A More Immediate Relation Between Justice and Faith?

Now that we have constantly portrayed charity in a mediating role at the heart of the relation between faith and justice, we want to turn to an effort of Jon Sobrino, a Jesuit from El Salvador, to find an even more direct and, in a sense, immediate relationship of justice to faith—as well as of faith to justice. He writes:

> We will try to show how the practice of justice concretizes the meaning of faith in deeds and how it makes possible the manifestation of the mystery of God at the very heart of historical action; how at the same time it causes to appear in history the most important aspects of that mystery **which would not be seen so easily through other forms of the practice of love.**[4]

It is worth the effort to follow this line of thought a bit further and to evaluate how Sobrino demonstrates his conclusion.

By our very practice of justice, Sobrino writes, we reach God as mystery.

> The always-greater being of God can be reached by an extrapolation which leads us to his unlimited reality, by means of philosophical considerations on created being or through experiences of an aesthetic, intellectual or sapiential kind issuing in admiration, leading on to a look—towards, a gaze which goes beyond that which, in a strict sense, is reached experientially. In the practice of justice the nature of divine transcendence appears in a different manner, a manner more radical in fact. The mystery of God-always-greater is reached through the **greater** which is found in the demand to humanize humankind, to re-create it. . . . The process of being ever more just to the other and the experience one has of a priori limitlessness of the "more," the impossibility for the one who practices justice to determine how far its demands go mediates the experience of God-ever-greater. . . . Favoring the poor and the effort to enter into solidarity with them presuppose a process of impoverishing of self [*proprio empobrecimiento*] and, through that, of a kind

---

[4] Jon Sobrino, S.J., "La promoción de la justicia come exigencia esencial del mensaje evangelico," *Diakonia*, no. 12 (December 1979): 45, translation mine.

of connaturality with the reality of God Himself, such as He appears in the Scriptures: one sees God as partial to poverty hidden in the little ones. One finds a path to God-ever-greater and transcendent through contact with the God who is always smaller, hidden in the little ones, crucified on the cross of Jesus as on the countless crosses of the oppressed of our time. (45f)

In the second place, Sobrino says, our approach to God represents a choice: for God and against everything else. This approach is realized in our choosing between two alternatives. We cannot serve two masters. We must be with Jesus or against him. Those who lose their life find it. So, he explains, the practice of justice already places us in such a situation of choice between the two alternatives of justice and injustice: "giving life to others or dealing death to them." In the practice of justice, we face a **basic** and discriminating choice: God himself (completely other) or else false gods. Ultimately we must choose between these alternatives.

In the third place, Sobrino says:

> The experience of the mystery of God is not reducible to self-knowledge left to itself, but it brings with it the factual situation of knowing that one is "commanded" by it. From the point of view of philosophical reflection itself, it is clear that God has the power to command and to command in a totally demanding way. . . . So the practice of justice concretizes, radicalizes and makes completely clear the demand of God and the call to respond to that demand with a sense of urgency. (48)

Sobrino, on the other hand, points to the attitude of the person who is ready to give his life so that others may live; there too, in the negation itself, there is an "**affirmation** of the mystery of God" (49). Further, Sobrino points to that quality of the mystery of God which is its hiddenness: obscurity, silence, each felt at times as more powerful than God's word. In sum, the experience of God is wrested from incredulity, in the sense that one believes **in spite of** ever-so-many temptations and objections. So, he says, the results of this search for justice are themselves often negative. The scandal of the victory of the tyrant over its victim is not far from the perception of the mystery of God's powerlessness, of the wisdom of the cross.

In brief, it appears that the practice of justice leads to something radical, unlimited, as well as obscure, opening into the very ground of God himself, his infinity, his mystery. Indisputably, there is a

very interesting aspect to this consideration which is indeed similar
to the reflections of Fathers Kerber, Rahner and Zwiefelhofer. It
calls our attention to the love of God found in love for man. Further,
it is necessary to point out that, by speaking less explicitly of
"transcendentalism" than those three did, Sobrino runs the risk of
occasionally presenting us with a too immediate relation of justice to
faith, so much so that, when pushed to the extreme, it is the very
dimensions of the practice of justice which in his view are the
mystery of God or aspects of that mystery. In transcendentalism
there is no such direct inclusion of the one in the other; there is
solely the implication of the absolute in human acts, which remain
limited and finite so far as their dimension in history is concerned.

### No Omission of the Mediation of Charity

Be it as it may about this matter, it seems preferable in discussions
on exactly how faith is related to justice always to include the explicit mediation of charity. Certainly, charity is not realistically
understood and, indeed, is betrayed if from the very first justice is
not given its place. Again, it is true that justice speaks of rigor,
radicality, and persistence; so the practice of justice can make us
aware of certain aspects of the mystery of God, as Sobrino points out
so well. But is it not always necessary to point out explicitly that
the practice of justice, which is the form of charity, should always
rest in charity? Otherwise, do we not face the danger of reaching a
demanding and jealous God rather than the loving, pardoning, and
merciful One? Surely we are talking about a nuance in the thought
of Sobrino, a writer burning with passion for justice. But the nuance
is not without moment, and we should not dismiss as unimportant
the example of Decree 4 itself in its more important doctrinal
passages about the mediation of charity. In particular, it is always
good to keep in mind, heart, and speech what the decree says about
"the conversion to the love of neighbor and, **therefore,** to the demands of justice" (no. 28 [77]), or about the "perfect justice of the
Gospel which shines out" in pardon towards those who have injured
us or shown us hostility, in "reconciliation" and "mercy" (no. 18
[67]). To summarize, we can say that the practice of justice which
charity demands truly leads us to faith, just as faith calls for it in
turn.

# PART III

# WORK OF THE CHURCH, WORK OF THE SOCIETY OF JESUS

# Chapter Nine

## EVANGELIZATION AND THE PROMOTION OF JUSTICE

C learly, we cannot establish any relation between evangelization and the promotion of justice unless first of all there exists an intrinsic and essential relation between faith and justice. We have seen that there is such a relation, essentially through the mediation of charity. But, inversely, the fact of the existence of the second relation does not say everything about the first one. Actually, we now enter the domain of concrete actions. The Church is within humanity but is not humanity in its entirety, so evangelization is a relatively specific task. Can it also include other tasks, including that of promoting justice?

The reflection of the entire Church on this question was very much sought at the very moment that the Society of Jesus was adopting Decree 4. As we have already noted, the 1971 synod of bishops had discussed this point in its document *Justice in the World,* and the synod of 1974 had just completed its study of the range of problems posed by evangelization. In 1975 Pope Paul VI published his encyclical *Evangelii nuntiandi.* To say nothing of the papal statements directed to the Society of Jesus, these documents all throw light on and locate what the general congregation itself says in its Decree 4.

### In Decree 4

Now what did General Congregation 32 itself say? It used very clear formulas. We have already seen them; but it is useful to reread them here. "The promotion of justice is an absolute requirement" of "the service of the faith (D. 4, no. 2 [48]). "Service of the faith" is a term very close to "evangelization." Again, the "struggle for justice" is included in "the struggle for faith" (D. 2, no. 2 [12]). "The promotion of justice is an integral part of evangelization" (D. 4, no. 30

[79]). "The promotion of justice is an integral part of the **priestly** service of the faith" (no. 18, [67], emphasis added). This is a more specific statement because it looks to priestly ministry. Finally, the congregation used the word "evangelization" itself as follows: ". . . evangelization is proclamation of that faith which is made operative in love of others; the promotion of justice is indispensable to it" (no. 28 [77], citing Gal. 5:6 and Eph. 4:15). Nor should we pass over in silence the remark "[I]t will not be possible to bring Christ to people or to proclaim His Gospel effectively unless a firm decision is taken to devote ourselves to the promotion of justice" (no. 27 [76]).

## The Synod of 1971

In its official documents the Church clearly confirms these points of view. At the same time, true enough, it nuanced them, especially at the synod of 1975. It is also more explicit than is Decree 4 in its letter concerning the difference of roles, especially between laity and priests, who share the work of evangelization.

Let us first of all investigate the relationship of these elements. We recall the formula of the synod of 1971: "Action on behalf of justice and a participation in the transformation of the world" are "a constitutive dimension of the preaching of the Gospel or, in other words, of the Church's mission for the redemption of the human race and its liberation from every oppressive situation" (*Justice in the World*, no. 6). This way of putting things, according to the synod, is supported by the very example of Christ Himself.

> In his preaching he proclaimed the fatherhood of God towards all men and the intervention of God's justice on behalf of the needy and oppressed (Luke 6:21–23). In this way he identified himself with his "least brethren," as he stated: "As you did it to one of the least of my brethren, you did it to me" (Matt. 25:40). (no. 31)

Then, turning to the proper mission of the Church, the synod declared:

> The Church has received from Christ the mission of preaching the Gospel message, which contains a call to man to turn away from sin to the love of the Father, universal brotherhood and a consequent demand for justice in the world. [The Church has the duty to] proclaim justice on the social, national and international level, and

to denounce instances of injustice, when the fundamental rights of man and his very salvation demand it." (no. 36)

Following these statements, which already outline the necessary distinctions, the Church approaches the question of promotion of justice from a very specific point of view, as the following illustrates:

The Church, indeed, is not alone responsible for justice in the world; however, she has a proper and specific responsibility which is identified with her mission of giving witness before the world of the need for love and justice contained in the Gospel message, a witness to be carried out in Church institutions themselves and in the lives of Christians. (no. 36)

The specific mission, then, of the Church is to give **witness to the need** for love and justice contained in the Christian message, not to do everything by itself in the struggle for justice.

On the other hand, the Church as a community stands before the world and it presents itself, officially in a way, as a community whose members are engaged in daily life. Immediately a certain sharing of tasks results. "Of itself it does not belong to the Church, insofar as she is a religious and hierarchical community, to offer concrete solutions in the social, economic and political spheres for justice in the world. Her mission involves defending and promoting the dignity and fundamental rights of the human person" (no. 37).

From their side,

the members of the Church, as members of society, have the same right and duty to promote the common good as do other citizens. Christians ought to fulfil their temporal obligations with fidelity and competence. They should act as a leaven in the world, in their family, professional, social, cultural and political life. . . . While in such activities they generally act on their own initiative without involving the responsibility of the ecclesiastical hierarchy, in a sense they do involve the responsibility of the Church whose members they are. (no. 38)

Truly a distinction sufficiently loose and relative, as we have just seen, since it is the same persons—Christians involved in their work and acting on their own responsibility in the world and "under the influence of the Gospel and the teaching of the Church" (no. 38) —who at one and the same time make up the community of the Church. Members of the hierarchy are more distinct, representing in a more formal way the community-Church. Even in daily life, bishops to a greater extent exercise responsibility in the Church.

From all angles it always remains true that promotion of justice is a part of evangelization, whatever the distinctions.

## In "Evangelii nuntiandi"

The whole question was taken up again in 1975 by Pope Paul VI in his *Evangelii nuntiandi (On Evangelization in the Modern World)*. He spoke expressly about "human promotion," not about "promotion of justice," but the latter is clearly one element of the former.

In the third part of the document, entitled "The Content of Evangelization," Paul VI begins by clearly specifying the heart of the message, essential if it is to be the Christian message.

> To evangelize is first of all to bear witness, in a simple and direct way, to God revealed by Jesus Christ, in the Holy Spirit; to bear witness that in His Son God has loved the world—that in His Incarnate Word He has given being to all things and has called men to eternal life. . . .
>
> Evangelization will also always contain—as the foundation, center, and at the same time, summit of its dynamism—a clear proclamation that, in Jesus Christ, the Son of God made man, who died and rose from the dead, salvation is offered to all men, as a gift of God's grace and mercy. And not an immanent salvation, meeting material or even spiritual needs, restricted to the framework of temporal existence and completely identified with temporal desires, hopes, affairs and struggles, but a salvation which exceeds all these limits in order to reach fulfillment in a communion with the one and only divine Absolute. . . .
>
> Consequently evangelization cannot but include the prophetic proclamation of a hereafter, man's profound and definitive calling, in both continuity and discontinuity with the present situation. . . . The preaching likewise—and this is always urgent—of the search for God Himself through prayer which is principally that of adoration and thanksgiving, but also through communion with the visible sign of the encounter with God which is the Church of Jesus Christ [and with the sacraments of that Church]. (*Evangelii nuntiandi*, no. 27f)

With this once established, Pope Paul VI felt comfortable in speaking about the relation between evangelization and human promotion.

> But evangelization would not be complete if it did not take account of the unceasing interplay of the Gospel and of man's concrete life, both personal and social. . . .
>
> Between evangelization and human advancement—development and liberation—there are in fact profound links. (nos. 29, 31)

Let us also reread the continuation of his thought, though we have already quoted it at the beginning of this work.

> These include links of an anthropological order, because the man who is to be evangelized is not an abstract being but is subject to social and economic questions. They also include links in the theological order, since one cannot dissociate the plan of creation from the plan of Redemption. The latter plan touches the very concrete situations of injustice to be combated and of justice to be restored. They include links of the eminently evangelical order, which is that of charity: how in fact can one proclaim the new commandment without promoting in justice and in peace the true, authentic advancement of man? (no. 31)

Taught by crises which had developed here and there in the last decades, however, Paul VI insisted upon the following:

> We must not ignore the fact that many, even generous Christians who are sensitive to the dramatic questions involved in the problem of liberation, in their wish to commit the Church to the liberation effort are frequently tempted to reduce her mission to the dimensions of a simply temporal project. They would reduce her aims to a man-centered goal; the salvation of which she is the messenger would be reduced to material well-being. Her activity, forgetful of all spiritual and religious preoccupation, would become initiatives of the political or social order. (no. 32)

"But if this were so," the Pope exclaimed, "the Church would lose her fundamental meaning," her originality. She would lose her authority to proclaim "freedom as in the name of God" (no. 32).

> The Church links human liberation and salvation in Jesus Christ, but she never identifies them, because she knows through revelation, historical experience and the reflection of faith that not every notion of liberation is necessarily consistent and compatible with an evangelical vision of man, of things and of events; she knows too that in order that God's kingdom should come it is not

enough to establish liberation and to create well-being and development. (no. 35)

Do we not find an insistence here on the necessary distinctions
as well as on essential linkages? Perhaps. It was the experience of
the previous few years that elicited all this attention from the Pope.
With the passage of still more years, we should once again see both
the distinctions and the links.

Moreover, in a positive vein, Paul VI offered the Church, especially as an official community, the following program:

> She is trying more and more to encourage large numbers of Chris-
> tians to devote themselves to the liberation of men. She is provid-
> ing these Christian "liberators" with the inspiration of faith, the
> motivation of fraternal love, a social teaching which the true
> Christian cannot ignore and which he must make the foundation of
> his wisdom and of his experience in order to translate it concretely
> into forms of action, participation and commitment. . . . The Church
> strives always to insert the Christian struggle for liberation into
> the universal plan of salvation which she herself proclaims. (no. 38)

For their part, the Pope said, the laity should find that "[t]heir own
field of evangelizing activity is the vast and complicated world of
politics, society and economics, and in the world of culture, the
sciences, and the arts also," as well as the world of their families
and professional activities.

### John Paul II Takes a Position of His Own

It was in turn John Paul II who insisted as firmly as possible on the
specificity of the role of priests and religious in evangelization. We
have already seen his position in the remarks he addressed directly
to the Society of Jesus: There is room to make up for the absence of
others in exceptional cases, but this is less necessary today than in
the past (his reason, it seems, is that lay men and women now have
a higher degree of culture than in the past); normally, however, the
priest is to work for the promotion of justice by animating and form-
ing lay men and women rather than by personally assuming responsibilities which are linked directly to the promotion of justice.

We have already had occasion to reread the Pope's 1980 address
to the priests at Rio de Janeiro, a text which he recalled in his

February 27, 1982, remarks to the Jesuits. In 1979 he had already said these words to the priests and religious of Mexico:

> You are spiritual guides, entrusted with the task of working to orient the hearts of the faithful, to make them better, to convert them so that they may live for love of God and neighbor and serve the promotion and dignity of all men. . . .
>
> You are priests and religious, not social directors, political leaders or functionaries of a temporal power.[1]

It is true that John Paul II was very actively involved in the defense of human rights and freedom and in the denunciation of many forms of injustice—in the promotion of justice, consequently. Moreover, in speaking to the Jesuits on February 27, 1982, he clearly recalled that "the Church considers the promotion of justice to be an integral part of evangelization." A few lines further on he speaks of "a necessary concern for justice." The one problem for him, then, was the clarification of exactly which roles are proper to priests and religious and which usually lie within the competence of the laity. The most general statement of General Congregation 32 on the promotion of justice as an absolute demand of the service of the faith, as an integral part of evangelization, and as a necessary aspect of the proclamation of Jesus Christ—these are solidly established points. Moreover, General Congregation 33 affirmed them anew.

## Clarifications

Now it is likewise clear that the link between evangelization and the promotion of justice is by no means a superficial one. In this regard, it is not enough to say that the commitment to justice provides credibility for the messenger of the Gospel in a world where the proclamation of justice is seen as having **value.** Like the bishops in the 1971 synod, we must in truth refer to the way in which Christ himself had acted or, as Paul VI expressed it, to the unity of our love for God and for our neighbor and to the bonds of fraternity based on the resemblance of all to the one we all address as Father. This teaching would become crucial in the years immediately ahead; for the exaggerations and the reactions which they

---

[1] *Acta Apostolicæ Sedis* 71, no. 3 (Feb. 28, 1979): 182, no. 7f.

necessarily provoked—along with unauthorized interpretations— threatened to turn people away from contributing to the promotion of justice required by evangelization. Because it was necessary to insist that this was not the whole of evangelization, some were in danger of treating it as a secondary element or totally neglecting it. General Congregation 33, after studying the effects of Decree 4, rightly stated that "neither a disincarnate spiritualism nor a merely secular activism truly serves the integral Gospel message" (D. 1, no. 33 [36]).

### *In Practice*

In what spheres was the desired equilibrium to be sought and carefully guarded? First of all, assuredly, in the life and activity of every Christian, but also in the life of all who preach the Gospel and in the way they parcel out their time and activities. There might indeed be a certain specialization among those evangelizing; but no one, not even a bishop, could entirely turn over to others his responsibilities to serve the faith through clear and direct teaching or to promote justice.

Indeed, here too there was a well-established teaching which Decree 4 proposed. The problem here was not so much undertaking or promoting specific activities under the name "social apostolate"; rather it was taking steps to make the promotion of justice a dimension of every apostolate. Moreover, there could be no Jesuit social action "unless we also preach Jesus Christ and the mystery of reconciliation He brings (D. 4, 27 [76]). Promoting justice, clearly presenting our faith, and proceeding toward a personal meeting with Christ: these are three inseparable elements of the whole of our apostolate, according to Decree 4 (no. 51 [100]). So neither "three distinct fields" nor "three apostolic sectors"!

Difficult indeed. Really, however, it is clear that anyone wishing to bring the good news of the Gospel to others and to invite them to believe should teach by example, be charitable towards the neighbor, and be just in all relations with others. But is more needed? Must there be an express commitment to justice that goes beyond the fact of showing oneself to be just in situations where one is personally involved? Furthermore, could it not be said that the essential task of the evangelizer is, without too much concern for other matters, to evoke belief in others? To lead others, that is, to give themselves confidently to God revealed in Christ, as to a Father who loves all men and women, and thus to arouse by word and example attitudes of charity, justice, reconciliation, and mercy, so characteristic of the Gospel. Thus alerted, people would of their own initiative take up the promotion of justice. Should the teacher of the Gospel do more by involving himself in the tasks—often so absorbing and complex—of promoting justice? Does he not run the risk of going outside his own role or of becoming so involved in such tasks as no longer to be able to give enough time and energy to his own proper task or vocation?

In response, let us underline the fact that in this hypothetical question the one who brings the Gospel to others arouses "by **word** and **example**" attitudes of charity and justice. At least, this should always be found in evangelizing activity. Further, Christian preaching should always be complete. In the words of Decree 4, "fidelity to our apostolic mission requires that we propose the whole of Christian salvation and teach others to embrace it. Christian salvation consists in an undivided love of the Father and of the neighbor and of justice" (no. 28 [77]). Moreover, this should be carried on very concretely, thus arousing the other to the **demands** of justice (and of charity), insofar as this is necessary; for there are many who do not see, or whose view should be enlarged.

Let us add that this responsibility of preaching the whole Gospel already imposes a real and very heavy obligation on the evangelizer who finds himself confronting grave injustice that he cannot ignore without betrayal. This will not be effected without personal consequences, but these will be an example to others, just as was the life of Jesus at the dawning of our faith.

### Different Charisms

There is place for various kinds of discernment and for a diversity of charisms. In reference to preaching—understood as every manner of teaching of Christ's message, as well as every exchange of words between the evangelizer and others—we have already tried to explain that the commitment of the one evangelizing to promote justice or

fight against injustice **is not reducible** to the individual's personal
attitude toward the justice demanded of him in his or her own social
relations with others. The specific contribution to promoting justice
on the part of all who evangelize, whether individuals or groups,
such as religious congregations, will surely be many and varied.

What matters is that evangelizers not hold back because the
task is difficult, but that instead they seek and search anew to be
faithful to the incarnational realism to be found in the unity of the
tasks of promoting justice and of evangelizing or serving the faith.
This unity, it can be said, has become a common property of Jesuits
through Decree 4, just as it is a good shared by all in the Church as
a result of the episcopal synods of 1971 and 1974, as well as Paul
VI's exhortation *Evangelii nuntiandi*. A common good, reaffirmed by
John Paul II, who points to the human person as a "way" for the
Church.

In the next chapter we must still see how the Society of Jesus
for its part has taken up the question of its more specific contribution.

# Chapter Ten

## AN APPROPRIATE CHOICE FOR THE SOCIETY OF JESUS

I n the context of a demand that it contribute to the promotion of
justice in order to bring to completion the work of evangelization,
the Society of Jesus effectively made a choice which is appropriate for it. That is to say, it was not content to fall back on the
general teaching of the Church concerning all involved in evangelization, but really applied this teaching to itself in the light of its
own purposes and its distinct tradition. There would be no point in
discussing those aspects that refer only to the Society. We will,
however, carry on our reflections in this chapter in the conviction
that the deliberations of the Jesuits can be of interest to other
apostolic forces in the Church, including the laity and religious men
and women working for similar apostolic purposes. At the same time
we will keep in mind the differences among these groups.

### Traditional Purposes of the Society of Jesus

The choice made by the Jesuits may be surprising. For were they
not known above all for their contribution to spiritual formation and
to the intellectual apostolate? "What is a Jesuit?" Pope Paul VI
asked on December 3, 1974, at the beginning of General Congregation 32. His answer, in sum, was: "He is a spiritual leader, an edu-
cator of his contemporaries in Catholic life, within . . . his proper
role as a priest and as an apostle" (*Documents,* 529). In the history
of the Church, the Society is seen in a special way as a school of
spirituality. "School" in a broad sense, certainly, in which discernment of the divine will for life in the world—professional, social, and
political—is central. Why, then, did Decree 4 take shape with its emphasis on promotion of justice so particularly underlined?

The goal of the Society is set forth especially in the "Formula of
the Institute," a document approved by the Pope, who remains

responsible for it. In this document it is clear that the Society's main purpose and principal task is

> to strive especially for the defense and propagation of the faith, and for the progress of souls in Christian life and doctrine, by means of public preaching, lectures, and any other ministrations whatsoever of the word of God, and further, by means of the Spiritual Exercises, the education of children and unlettered persons in Christianity, and the spiritual consolation of Christ's faithful through hearing confessions and administering the other sacraments. (D. 4, no. 17 [66], citing the Formula of the Institute, [3], [1])

Perhaps what follows has not always received sufficient attention:

> The Society is also established to work in reconciling the estranged, in holily assisting and serving those who are found in prisons and hospitals, and indeed in performing any other works of charity, according to what will seem expedient for the glory of God and the common good. (no. 17 [66], citing the Formula of the Institute, [3], [1])

This second finality ("The Society is **also** established . . .") was by no means a matter of chance. On the contrary, the involvement of St. Ignatius and his first companions in works and activities directed toward healing every kind of suffering, especially in Rome, had from its origins been a characteristic trait of their kind of life. As we have already seen, St. Ignatius came to the aid of the unfortunate, assisted prostitutes to escape from their situation, worked incessantly to bring an end to unjust discrimination against Jews, obliged his companions who had been sent to the Council of Trent to help the poor in hospitals as well. This sort of experience certainly did not disappear from Jesuit life.

As they reread the two major quotations given just above, the members of General Congregation 32 affirmed, "This primordial statement remains for us a normative one" (D. 4, no. 17 [66]). On the basis of that statement, they reached the conclusion that today the mission of the Society should be "service of the faith and promotion of justice."

## The Promotion of Justice Is Very Much in Accord with These Purposes

But in certain quarters this question has arisen: Does the promotion of justice correspond to the Society's second purpose, which we have just reread? Does not the Formula of Pope Julius III speak of charity more than of justice? There is surely a nuance involved. It can be said, as we have just recalled in the words of both Pope Paul VI and Father Arrupe, that charity is always greater than justice. But every call of charity to which Jesuits should respond is not thereby the same as a call of justice. On the other hand, if we understand justice as we should in the light of clarifications given here, the promotion of justice as explained in Decree 4 corresponds well, we believe, to the second finality of the Society described in the Formula of Pope Julius III. The expression has the advantage of being realistic, as well as demanding. Surely, we must correctly understand its meaning: it is not so much charity as the demand for justice itself—so charity in the sense of work to bring about justice with all its demands. We have also recalled that the justice to be promoted is the "perfect justice of the Gospel," calling for one to work to one's limits as God himself does, thus turning the unjust and sinful person into someone just and lovable. Further, justice is to be promoted in the spirit of the Beatitudes, a spirit of reconciliation. If we understand it in this sense, we can then say that the promotion of justice corresponds very well to the intention expressed in the Formula of the Society's Institute. Assuredly, justice should always be understood in this way.

It is no less important that we keep in mind the "priestly" character, fundamental for every type of service of the Society, including its contribution to the promotion of justice. Immediately after citing the Formula of Pope Julius, the congregation continued as follows: "The mission of the Society today is the **priestly** service of the faith, an apostolate whose aim is to help people become more open toward God and more willing to live according to the demands of the Gospel" (D. 4, no. 18 [67], emphasis added). To live in accord with the Gospel, we read immediately after, implies seeking for justice, but it is clear that every effort that Jesuits make to this end is an "apostolic" task, better still, a "priestly service." This has much to do with the concrete modalities, about which we will speak in the following chapters. If we keep these clarifications in mind, we are on solid ground in linking the Society's contribution to the promotion of justice to its second finality as expressed in the Formula of its Institute.

### *In Line Too with the Spiritual Exercises*

In the second place, we can say that the kind of approach to our day-to-day life which is typical of the Spiritual Exercises likewise leads us to the choice made in General Congregation 32, as the congregation itself explains. The characteristic approach to which St. Ignatius has formed Jesuits consists in the following: to see and contemplate

> "how the Three Divine Persons look down upon the whole expanse or circuit of all the earth, filled with human beings" and decide that "the Second Person should become man to save the human race"; after that, to look into how "they themselves might respond to the call of Christ and to work for the establishment of His Kingdom." The three Divine Persons see men and women "one after the other, with such great diversity in dress and in manners of acting. Some are white, some black; some at peace, and some at war; some weeping, some laughing; some well, some sick; some coming into the world, some dying, etc." (D. 4, nos. 14 [63] and 19 [68], quoting *Spiritual Exercises,* 102, 106)

General Congregation 32 says that Jesuits today, like the Divine Persons in that contemplation, should "hear anew the call of Christ dying and rising in the anguish and aspirations of men and women" (no. 19 [68]).

What today determines the choice made by the Society in Decree 4 is the vision of humanity suffering both from a deep spiritual upheaval, often indeed from spiritual suffocation, and also from great social tribulations or enormous injustices. Between these two poles of the human condition, moreover, there are links. On the one hand, we find in many real ignorance of God, though often accompanied by a thirst for him, and in others the loss of a sense of God, overturning of values, secularization (nos. 4f [50f], 24f [73f]). On the other hand, a world "increasingly interdependent but, for all that, divided by injustice" (no. 6 [52]), where "it is within human power to make the world more just—but we do not really want to" (no. 27

[76]); "millions of men and women in our world, specific people with names and faces, who are suffering from poverty and hunger, from the unjust distribution of wealth and resources and from the consequences of racial, social, and political discrimination" (no. 20 [69]).

The conclusion to all this: Jesus Christ must be proclaimed if we wish to rescue humankind from this situation of blockage brought about by profound selfishness, which makes impossible a victory over poverty and injustice, even when the means to overcome them are available. At the same time, in this situation the promotion of evangelical justice must go hand in hand with proclaiming the Gospel.

> Hence there can be no promotion of justice in the full and Christian sense unless we also preach Jesus Christ and the mystery of reconciliation He brings. It is Christ who, in the last analysis, opens the way to the complete and definitive liberation of mankind for which we long from the bottom of our hearts. Conversely, it will not be possible to bring Christ to people or to proclaim His Gospel effectively unless a firm decision is taken to devote ourselves to the promotion of justice. (no. 27 [76])

This combination of spiritual need and social misery, on the other hand, is explained as follows:

> At the same time, people today are somehow aware that their problems are not just social and technological, but personal and spiritual. They have a feeling that what is at stake here is the very meaning of man: his future and his destiny. People are hungry: hungry not just for bread but for the Word of God. (no. 21 [70])

In summary, we can say that contemplating the world as the Divine Persons do and in accord with what Ignatius taught us to do leads us still today to offer ourselves to help brothers and sisters in their distress, which is fundamentally spiritual but at the same time always temporal. There is need, then, of a vision of the human person and all his aspirations but at the same time in the concrete reality of his situation—white, black, at peace, at war. For the Jesuit schooled so to view things, the promotion of justice is truly, and has a very particular claim to be, an integral part of the service of the faith for which he offers himself. He must first meet his fellows in that unity which is theirs, a unity, however, which does not at all limit his basic concern for the spiritual.

## *A Function of the Society of Jesus in Its Relation to Unbelief*

Now there are still other special reasons for Jesuits today to give such attention to the promotion of justice. Those reasons derive from the recommendation made by Pope Paul VI and his successors, namely, that they struggle against unbelief and bring assistance to nonbelievers and those threatened by nonbelief.

> What is at stake here is the fruitfulness of all our apostolic endeavors, and notably of any coherent attempt to combat atheism. The injustice that racks our world in so many forms is, in fact, a denial of God in practice, for it denies the dignity of the human person, the image of God, the brother or sister of Christ. (D. 4, no. 29 [78])

A struggle against one form of the denial of God should be accompanied by a struggle against injustice.

In another context, the general congregation went still further. On the one hand, it points out, many people reject the Gospel because they are involved in the injustices of the world. On the other hand, "the prevalence of injustice in a world where the very survival of the human race depends on men caring for and sharing with one another is one of the principal obstacles to belief: belief in a God who is justice because he is love" (D. 2, no. 7 [17]). The first of these two reasons obliges us to pay close attention to that kind of injustice found in everyday life when one tries to aid others to conversion. The second invites us to become involved in the struggle for justice in order to remove, as far as is possible for us, the scandal in question, clearly showing thereby that whoever fights for the cause of God is much concerned about justice even in the midst of so many injustices.

There is still another reason, similar to the preceding one: by committing themselves to a down-to-earth promotion of justice, people can make it clear that Christianity is not an opiate, as so many are inclined to believe.

> At a time when so many people are sparing no effort to put the world to rights without reference to God, our endeavor should be to show as clearly as we can that our Christian hope is not a dull opiate, but a firm and realistic commitment to make our world other than it is, to make it the visible sign of another world, the

sign—and pledge—of "a new heaven and a new earth." (D. 4, no. 30 [79])

In short, the call to fight atheism and to be accessible to atheists and to other types of nonbelievers, agnostics and the indifferent, for example, who are so numerous today, demands of the Society a particular alertness to injustice and a particular concern for its own contribution to the promotion of justice. This awareness and concern, however, must be correctly understood; for a wholly secular and simplistic kind of social activism would certainly say nothing about Jesus Christ and the God of Jesus Christ; nor would this kind of activism indicate to an unbeliever a possible answer to his basic questions concerning human destiny. What is needed is for a Jesuit to be perceived as one who is with reason haunted by such basic questions and at the same time very sensitive to other human needs. This is clearly stated in Decree 4, as the following shows:

> Finally, if the promotion of justice is to attain its ultimate end, it should be carried out in such a way as to bring men and women to desire and to welcome the eschatological freedom and salvation offered to us by God in Christ. . . . [Our work for justice] will respond to humanity's deepest yearnings, not just for bread and freedom, but for God and His friendship—a longing to be sons and daughters in His sight. (no. 33 [82])

It is, moreover, obvious that, if clarity of position and of behavior in relation to injustice makes it easier for unbelievers to draw near, it summons us also to other tasks and to other kinds of purification. For example, the general congregation says that it is urgent to "strive to find a new language, a new set of symbols" and to avoid any false or ambiguous images which may seem to "release man from his inalienable responsibilities" (no. 26 [75]).

Further, the congregation says:

> We must therefore review not only our commitment to justice but our effectiveness in communicating the truths which give it meaning and in bringing men to find Christ in their daily lives. We must attentively examine our efforts to strengthen the faith of those who already believe in Christ, taking into account the formidable forces that in our time tend to undermine that faith. We must subject to a similarly searching examination our efforts to bring the Gospel to unbelievers. (no. 52 [101])

So what is at stake is by no means a denial by the Society of its finality of service to the faith or to its tradition of being a spiritual school of concrete Christian life. Today, however, to achieve this very end there is need for a clear commitment to the promotion of justice. This is above all what Pope Paul VI, for example, had in mind in 1964 in speaking of at least some unbelievers.

> [Atheists] are sometimes men of great breadth of mind, impatient with the mediocrity and self-seeking which infect so much of modern society. They are quick to make use of sentiments and expressions found in our Gospel, referring to the brotherhood of man, mutual aid, and human compassion. Shall we not one day be able to lead them back to the Christian sources of these moral values?[1]

These, then, are some of the characteristics of the apostolic purposes of Jesuits. Certainly, they do not sharply distinguish them from other apostolic bodies, but they surely oblige Jesuits to clearly and strongly emphasize the promotion of justice in all their works, their various forms of witness, and in the image they give of themselves. Clearly, not enough has yet been done to live out this obligation in practice.

---

[1] *Ecclesiam suam,* in *The Pope Speaks* 10 (1964): 287, no. 104.

# Chapter Eleven

## CLOSENESS TO AND SOLIDARITY WITH THE POOR

n Decree 4 the Jesuits were not satisfied with a general statement, one expanding on the importance of the promotion of justice
in the Society's overall apostolate. We find in that decree an
attention to details regarding different conditions and individual
aspects of that choice, especially the following: identification and
solidarity with the poor, use of social analysis, participation in the
work of transforming structures, and even the political implications
of the latter. For this reason, therefore, the decree is not lacking in
a certain newness, and more than one question has arisen in the
course of its being put into practice. So it will be interesting to
decide at this point also what has been solidly achieved after eight
years, as well as to indicate those points demanding further research or involving controversy.

In this chapter we will consider two requests found in Decree 4,
the first regarding closeness to or identification with the poor; the
second, solidarity with them. This does not mean to say that the two
are identical or that poverty and an unjust situation are completely
identical. Rather, solidarity with the poor stems from the same motivation, the desire to be close to and share with the poor, a desire
which also urges one to become part of their life.

### The Need for Greater Identification with Others

First of all, let us take up Decree 4's stance on identification with
others. Clearly the main idea is quite simple: Those who hope to
contribute to the promotion of justice must be acquainted at first
hand with situations of injustice, and by means of real and immediate experience, grow in the ability to understand the demands of
justice. We will see that this is not all that is needed, but nothing
else can replace it. Knowledge through firsthand experience is

needed, and to that end the congregation strongly recommended greater closeness to and identification with others. Both knowledge and love are needed.

In Decree 4 identification with the lot of others is still more deeply rooted—in the Divine Persons' own awareness of the concrete conditions of human life, as presented by Ignatius in his contemplation on the Incarnation. Second, it is rooted in the need to be close to people as a necessary condition for preaching the Gospel, which "should be preached with fresh vigor" (no. 21 [70]).

In the third place, identification with others is based on the "missionary" tradition of the Society of Jesus and its characteristic openness to different cultures (no. 55 [104]). In his talk of December 3, 1974, did not Pope Paul VI praise those Jesuits who have been—and today still are—"at the crossroads of ideologies, in the front line of social conflict, [where] there has been and there is confrontation between the deepest desires of man and the perennial message of the Gospel . . ."?[1] This notion enlarges, it is true, what is meant by close proximity to the neighbor, but not without reason.

In contrast to this need for nearness to one's neighbor, as we have seen from the first pages of this book, the congregation stated that too often Jesuits stand at a distance from the concrete life of their brothers and sisters and, moreover, from situations of unbelief as well as injustice. For this reason they require closeness to the neighbor in order to come into contact with either unbelief or injustice. How "many . . . can no longer be reached by the ministries exercised through [typical Jesuit] works and institutions!" (no. 24 [73]). How many are there who do not yet know Jesus Christ and do not have the opportunity to meet messengers who will speak to others about him!

> Too often we are insulated from any early contact with unbelief and with the hard, everyday consequences of injustice and oppression. As a result we run the risk of not being able to hear the cry for the Gospel as it is addressed to us by the men and women of our time. . . . Are we ready, with discernment and with reliance on a community which is alive and apostolic, to bear witness to the Gospel in

---

[1] *Documents,* 527; see also GC 32, D. 4, no. 19 [68].

the painful situations where our faith and our hope are tested by unbelief and injustice? (no. 35 [84])

In truth, what is at stake is not always as much as that; sometimes it is enough to be no longer "protected" as one has been from "the simple life and its day-to-day concerns" (no. 49 [89]).

On the other hand, being present only for a short time is not enough. For example, as far as the poor are concerned, "[i]f we have the patience and the humility and the courage to walk with the poor, we will learn from what they have to teach us what we can do to help them" (no. 50 [99]).

A simple external change, such as taking up residence in a different place, does not suffice, for such a change may be artificial. What is needed is "a change in our habitual patterns of thought, a conversion of heart as well as of spirit" (no. 74 [123]). Young Jesuits, the congregation makes clear, should, at one time or other during their formative years, be expected to have an experience of living with the poor. Therefore, "the conditions of such an experience must be thought out carefully, so that it will be genuine, free of illusions, and productive of an inner conversion" (D. 6, no. 10 [142]).

During the course of General Congregation 32, the writer of this work was so deeply struck by the insistence on "insertion" and the indispensable experience of concrete life and thought—especially of the ways of thinking and feeling—that toward the close of 1975 he published a study on insertion as an essential part of the program of General Congregation 32.[2] We are speaking about a **hidden** decree, if one may so speak, because as a matter of fact there was no separate decree with that title, in contrast to those on promotion of justice, inculturation, and vowed poverty.

So, in the years following the congregation, there was much discussion about "insertion," particularly among those who were suffering from poverty and conditions of great injustice. As a matter of fact, a certain number of Jesuits went to live among such people. If

---

[2] Jean-Yves Calvez, S.J., "The Congregation and Closer Contact of Jesuits with Men," *Conferences on the Chief Decrees of the Jesuit General Congregation XXXII* (St. Louis: The Institute of Jesuit Sources, 1976), 147–59.

that was not always possible, attempts were made to encourage temporary experiences of this nature. "Exposure" was the term used to describe this experience of living in an environment far away from one's normal situation. In the United States experiences of this kind were systematically organized in poor areas of that country or in neighboring Latin American countries. Often such experiences were very demanding, not at all smacking of tourism. Such experiences, of course, had to be followed up perseveringly.

To be sure, there are limits, salutary ones, undoubtedly, to the kind of insertion religious might experience. First of all, because of their state as religious who have freely chosen celibacy; moreover, because usually they expect to live a community life. Decree 4, we have just seen, expressly spoke of the "support of living apostolic communities" as very necessary for Jesuits in surroundings profoundly marked by unbelief or even by injustice. In this connection, certainly, we should also keep in mind that it is possible to find apostolic communities beyond the circle of one's religious brothers or sisters.

A difficulty for Jesuits arises from the very demands of many apostolic works from which they cannot withdraw, even given the new attitudes arising from Decree 4. There was a period a few years ago when some Jesuits were scandalized to see some of their confreres residing outside the poorest parts of a city. A romantic view of reality was not totally absent, it seems, when certain Jesuits tried to move into very poor sections of the city only to sleep at night, while working all day long in the center of the city. It is more valuable sometimes for a person periodically to spend longer periods of time in sections very close to poor people, rather than try the impossible, or almost impossible—daily presence in a very poor quarter while carrying out one's duties elsewhere.

General Congregation 32 provided a properly nuanced norm about this matter.

> It will therefore be necessary for a larger number of us to share more closely the lot of families who are of modest means, who make up the majority of every country, and who are often poor and oppressed. Relying on the unity we enjoy with one another in the Society and our opportunity to share in one another's experience, we must all acquire deeper sensitivity from those Jesuits who have

chosen lives of closer approximation to the problems and aspirations of the deprived. (D. 4, no. 49 [98])

Certainly there is danger that a Jesuit may read too many nuances into his interpretations, thus running the risk of excusing himself from a true obligation. Nonetheless, General Congregation 33 in 1983 returned without hesitation to the importance of

deeper involvement in the lives of the people around us in order to hear "the joys and the hopes, the griefs and the anxieties of the people of this age, especially those who are poor or in any way afflicted"; a regular exposure to new situations of life and thought which oblige us to question our way of seeing and judging.[3]

### Solidarity with the Poor

The statement just cited is a reminder that insertion looks not only to the world of the poor or poorest but to that of any and all people. These we must understand very well, along with their social settings as well as their ways of thinking and feeling, including the way they relate to the world and to God. As a matter of fact, however, Decree 4 gives particular attention to insertion among the poor. Accordingly, insertion calls for "solidarity with the poor," a wider view which also gained a primary place in Decree 4.

Solidarity with the poor refers to all of life, not merely to particular tasks. In function of this solidarity, Decree 4 calls not only for a "review of our institutions and apostolic works" but insists that "it should be a characteristic of the life of all of us as individuals and a characteristic of our communities and institutions as well" (no. 48 [97]). It was in this global context that Decree 4 spoke of insertion.

A problem arises here. Solidarity with the poor is indisputably a very important evangelical and apostolic virtue, but poverty and a situation of injustice are not to be simply identified. To assert such an identity is to risk approaching a questionable Marxist position.

Decree 4 itself does not make many distinctions on the subject. It speaks at times of "solidarity with the poor" in virtue of the op-

---

[3] GC 33, D. 1, no. 41 [44], citing *Gaudium et spes,* no. 1.

tion for the promotion of justice, at times of "solidarity with those who lead a difficult life and are collectively oppressed," at times of those who share the life of the majority, "who are often poor and oppressed." Does it not seem, then, that every kind of poverty stems from oppression? But there are different kinds of poverty; for example, that of people who do not succeed in keeping up with the pace of industrial societies, or that of the physically handicapped. How does oppression or exploitation directly cause poverty of this nature? It is true, indeed, that one who becomes poor then easily falls prey to exploitation by reason of that condition. But identifying poverty with oppression risks falling into the dangerous, often very unjust attitude of trying to track down those thought to be responsible or culpable.

It is necessary, however, to establish a link between poverty and injustice, at least between inhuman levels of poverty (here we do not include the lot of those possessing only modest resources) and injustice. At the very least, a society desiring justice would not be able to abandon those who fall into poverty or remain there through no personal fault or only a slight one. Even if injustice is not at the root of every form of poverty, it would be unjust to let it continue if feasible ways to overcome it are at hand. Bearing these nuances in mind, we can say that there may always, or almost always, be a link between injustice and poverty. Hence, it follows that whoever wants to promote justice should stand in solidarity with the poor. Otherwise, it may well be that such a person is more interested in promoting an ideology rather than real justice. Actually, sometimes those who pretend to struggle for justice in the name of the Gospel seem to make distinctions between different kinds of poor people, and to want to concern themselves only with those who in their eyes seem able to join the "wave of the future" (in a revolution!). Such a stance is the opposite of true solidarity with the poor.

### *Preferential Options for the Poor*

Decree 4 did not include expressions such as "preferential option for the poor," which have become so common, for example, in Latin America. Instead, General Congregation 33 (1983) adopted this actual expression in the course of its consideration of Decree 4, directly relating it to the necessity of solidarity with the poor.

This expression could certainly be misunderstood, since it sometimes was taken in a directly political sense. Those who represented themselves as spokesmen for the poor, as well as some of the poor themselves, sometimes fell into such confusion. The expression, moreover, was sometimes taken in a one-sided sense to the exclusion of all else. General Congregation 33 offered this clarification on the point: "This option is a decision to love the poor preferentially because there is a desire to heal the whole human family. Such love, like Christ's own, excludes no one but neither does it excuse anyone from its demands"[4] (no. 48 [52]).

In the same way the Pope spoke to the Latin American bishops gathered at Rio de Janeiro on July 2, 1980: "It is with reason that you have made a preferential option in favor of the poor, an option assuredly not in an exclusive sense."[5] To the bishops of Brazil at Fortaleza a few days later, he addressed these remarks:

> The preferential option for the poor, which was clearly proclaimed at Puebla, is not an option which excludes. . . . A bishop is duty-bound to proclaim the entire Gospel to all, since all in effect should be "poor in spirit." Rather, this option is a call to be especially in solidarity with the little ones and the weak, with those who suffer and those who mourn, in order to help them always to realize in better ways their dignity as persons and children of God.[6]

---

[4] In examining the expression "preferential option for the poor" in 1980, the Vatican Congregation for Religious pointed out the need to find governing principles which would guarantee that both the choice of and involvement in activities for justice would "respond to the purpose and appropriate style of the Church's mission and, within it, of religious life" (*Religious and Human Promotion,* no. 4). A bit further on this document underlined the following: "The pastoral openness of the works and the preferential choice of the poor is the tendency which most marks Latin American religious life. Actually there are always more men and women religious to be found in marginal and difficult areas. . . . This choice does not presuppose the exclusion of others whoever they may be, but rather a preference for and an approach to the poor" (note 24).

[5] *Acta Apostolicæ Sedis* 72, no. 6 (Sept. 30, 1980): 873–80.

[6] *Acta Apostolicæ Sedis* 72, no. 6 (Sept. 30, 1980): 956, no. 6.9.

So in the end we are clearly led to the conclusion that a preferential option for the poor, including, possibly, solidarity with them, is not at all the same as the promotion of justice. It speaks of something far more extensive, for one must stand with the poor even when there is little that an individual can do to right the injustice that they experience. By being close to the poor, one does justice for them in some way or other, but not always in the way one at first intends. Helping the poor to rediscover and realize their dignity as humans and children of God, to use the words of Pope John Paul II just cited, is to do justice for them.

### Jesuit Implementation of the Option

All Jesuits, to be sure, do not easily carry into practice this evangelical preference for the poor, along with great attention not to exclude anyone, especially all those who suffer for reasons other than poverty, precisely by reason of other aspects of the apostolic goals given them by the Church. Often they must live out this preferential option for the poor without at the same time serving them directly. But at least they should always take care that in all their activities they do not contradict that preference, but always respect and carry it into practice when possible. In 1976, writing to the entire Society of Jesus, Father Arrupe directed some firm recommendations along these lines to Jesuits involved in the intellectual apostolate. Insofar as possible, he urged, when choosing topics for research and intellectual work, they should be alert to the possibility of coming to the assistance of the poorest; where they cannot live with the poor, they should at least give witness by their style of life to their preferential option. Father Arrupe continued:

> Still there are certain men who will be inspired to this sharing and at the same time to a life of intense intellectual work. I wish to encourage them. . . . Allowance being made for the legitimate needs that arise from the specific work of intellectuals, we are scarcely obliged to live in all respects like those with whom we work. Moreover, some intellectuals, of whatever persuasion, in this regard set a striking example that is far removed from prevailing middle-class standards. Could it be that we Jesuits are in arrears about desiring

to be identified with the poor Christ who himself is identified with the most defenseless?[7]

Despite the real difficulties encountered in certain situations, Jesuits almost always warmly welcomed the idea of the preferential option for the poor. As we have seen, the same could not always be said about the promotion of justice. Preference for the poor was certainly based on early Jesuit tradition. It suffices to recall the letter that St. Ignatius had his secretary, Polanco, write on August 7, 1547, to the Jesuits in Padua. In it we read:

> The poor are so important in God's view that it was for them that Jesus Christ was very specially sent. . . . Friendship with the poor enables one to become a friend of the eternal king. . . . "Blessed are the poor in spirit for the kingdom of heaven is theirs," for they have a right to the kingdom now. Not only are they themselves kings, but they enable others to participate in the kingdom.[8]

General Congregation 33 strongly insisted on the preferential option for the poor. "Directly or indirectly, this option should find some concrete expression in every Jesuit's life, in the orientation of our existing apostolic works, and in our choice of new ministries" (D. 1, no. 48 [52]). Its stress is perhaps somewhat different from that of General Congregation 32, but it repeated the close link between the three elements: promotion of justice, solidarity with the poor, and the preferential option for them. Though not identical, these three elements are interlinked, for solidarity with the poor in a completely realistic way presupposes commitment to bringing about the kind of justice which will relieve their condition.

---

[7] "The Intellectual Apostolate in the Framework of the Society's Options Today," *Acta Romana* 16 (1973–76): 1004, recalling GC 32, D. 4, no. 48 [97].

[8] St. Ignatius of Loyola, *Epistolæ et instructiones,* 1st series, Monumenta Ignatiana; vol. 22 of Monumenta Historica Societatis Iesu (Madrid, 1903; Rome, 1964) 1:573f. The scriptural references are to Matt. 5:5 and Luke 6:20.

# Chapter Twelve

## SOCIAL ANALYSIS, STRUCTURES, POLITICAL IMPLICATIONS

W e turn now to social analysis, action pointed towards transformation of structures, and the political implications of efforts to promote justice. In so doing, we arrive at the most controversial aspects of the program outlined in Decree 4. A sufficiently developed debate took place on all these matters, however, making it possible now to point out what here too is solidly established.

### *Social Analysis*

If nearness to the poor is a crucial factor leading to personal and experiential knowledge, Decree 4 did not urge it without at the same time recommending recourse to study and to reflection. Indeed, Decree 4 is quite insistent on the need for study, though this was not always understood when debate began on the subject of social analysis. "Are we ready to give ourselves to the demanding and serious study of theology, philosophy and the human sciences, which are ever more necessary if we are to understand and try to resolve the problems of the world?" (D. 4, no. 35 [84]).

In another context the term "analysis"—more precisely, "social analysis"—appears alongside terms which we have just read, terms denoting various fields of knowledge from theology to the human sciences. Analysis, as understood in this context, is a more direct approach to reality with application to a particular situation, though not without recourse to recognized scientific knowledge.

The most important passage from Decree 4 on this matter reads as follows:

> We cannot be excused from making the most rigorous possible political and social analysis of our situation. This will require the

utilization of the various sciences, sacred and profane, and of the various disciplines, speculative and practical, and all of this demands intense and specialized studies. (no. 44, [93])

It is abundantly clear that Jesuits should guard against being influenced by simple impressions and first reactions, as can occur when a sensitive person lacking the necessary preparation first encounters injustice.

Let it be clear first of all that the language employed in Decree 4 in no way permits the interpretation that Jesuits should take up only social analysis of whatever kind. This does not suffice nor does any other science all by itself. "Nothing should excuse us, either, from undertaking a searching discernment into our situation from the pastoral and apostolic point of view" (no. 44 [93]). The Jesuit approach, when all is said and done, can only be a religious one, looking to serve the faith or assist others from the viewpoint of Christian life and teaching, account being taken, to be sure, of all that social analysis can teach.

Despite this, some tended to oversimplify matters, reasoning somewhat as follows: Our apostolic mission demands a commitment to justice on our part, a share in the struggle against injustice; once we have received that mandate, we have no alternative other than to search out the causes of prevailing injustice, which we will discover by impartial and, if possible, scientific analysis. The hope was that this analysis would possibly lead at the same time to solutions. On such a tack, one quickly encounters the kind of social analysis put forward by Marxists. This is distinguished by its notable simplicity, reducing as it does every injustice to the same cause and at the same time indicating a remedy equally univocal. Besides, it passes itself off as "scientific," applying to that adjective a sense clearly different from the one regularly employed by recognized sciences.

Even apart from the difficulties found in Marxism, these Jesuits expected too much from this kind of analysis. Some deluded themselves here, thinking that it could be used without criteria based on values, with the help of laboratory methods only. The truth, of course, is that all social analysis begins and proceeds in the light of the particular values which one embraces. The questions which arouse one's interest, the groups to be investigated, and the questions to be posed derive from the investigator's values and criteria of value. From a Christian viewpoint, for example, the place accorded to human dignity, or the possibility of taking responsible action and of participating in the kind of social life which concerns a person will count for much, as will such factors as the level of satisfaction which more material elements can provide. Such material elements, however, are almost the single determining factor in certain other approaches.

From the same Christian point of view, whoever is trying to ferret out the causes of situations which are inhuman will always try to find the deviations of human freedom, and no one will be satisfied with pointing out nameless mechanisms. In seeking remedies such a person will trust in persuasion more than in constraint alone, even if he does not always exclude the latter. One will never despair of the possibility of conversion of heart and, through that, of behavior. Furthermore, one will see that in every political judgment there is an element of the variable, even if that judgment is supported by scientific conclusions; so, instead of seeking to impose in simplistic fashion some truth, whatever it may be, one will tend to pave the way for meeting the "other" and for that kind of mutual recognition which is able to flower in some new form of understanding, imperfect perhaps, but better than that obtainable by force. So it is clear that a whole view of humanity and of human society is at stake in the way in which social analysis is carried on.

## On the Use of Marxist Social Analysis

With reference to Marxism in particular, Father Arrupe felt obliged to speak out and clearly show that not every form of social analysis is compatible with a Christian view of things. As early as the 1978 congregation of procurators, he took the following position in his report on the state of the Society:

> Without closing ourselves to the good that can be found in Marxism and without excluding the possibility of dialogue and even of a certain critical collaboration with groups and movements of Marxist inspiration, it is evident that the commitment of some Jesuits to Marxism as such and their public declarations of support for its ideology are unacceptable and cause scandal and confusion, not

only for those suffering oppression and persecution under Marxist regimes, but also for many others.[1]

Later, in a letter of 1980 to the provincials of Latin America on Marxist analysis, he went into greater detail on this point. He took special pains to reply to those who were asking whether at the heart of Marxism one could not distinguish between social analysis on the one hand and, on the other, the philosophy linked with the antireligious ideology, and thus accept the first while discarding the second. As one might have foreseen, Father Arrupe was aware that social analysis is never neutral when there is question of values, and that what was currently presented as Marxist social analysis implied a certain number of presuppositions characteristic of Marxist ideology and contrary to Christian convictions. So he responded in the following terms:

> It seems to me that in our analysis of society, we can accept a certain number of methodological viewpoints which, to a greater or lesser extent, arise from marxist analysis, as long as we do not attribute an exclusive character to them. For instance, an attention to economic factors, to property structures, to economic interests which motivate this or that group; or again, a sensibility to the exploitation that victimizes entire classes, attention to the role of class struggle in history (at least, of many societies), attention to ideologies which can camouflage for vested interests and even for injustice.
>
> In practice, however, the adoption of marxist analysis is rarely the adoption of only a method or an "approach." Usually it means accepting the substance of the explanations Marx provided for the social reality of his time. . . .[2]

As particularly unacceptable Father Arrupe singled out the following elements: historical materialism with its tendency to reductionism, especially in what concerns the faith; the generalization of the theory of class struggle as explaining all of social history; especially, the idea of class struggle to be used as a strategic principle, that is, as a struggle understood (quite paradoxically, it is true)

---

[1] Father Arrupe's first address to the congregation, *Acta Romana* 17, no. 2 (1978): 456f.

[2] Letter to the provincials of Latin America, *Acta Romana* 18, no. 1 (1980): 340.

as the "privileged means for doing away with struggle." He concluded his reflections as follows:

> In brief, although marxist analysis does not directly imply ac-
> ceptance of marxist philosophy as a whole—and still less of dialec-
> tical materialism as such—as it is normally understood, it implies
> in fact a concept of human history in contradiction with the chris-
> tian view of man and society and leading to strategies which
> threaten Christian values and attitudes. . . .

> To adopt therefore not just some elements or some methodologi-
> cal insights, but marxist analysis as a whole, is something we can-
> not accept. (342f)

So, even apart from every philosophical proposition based on
theism, Marxist social analysis carries with it presuppositions and
convictions derived from an understanding of the human person
which are very alien to the Christian view. For the Christian,
Marxism relies excessively on "system" and "structure" instead of
on "freedom"; on "opposition" or "contradiction" rather than on
mutual recognition of different forms of freedom. To sum up, on the
one hand there is little confidence in man, and this indeed in a view
which sets out to establish such confidence; on the other, there exists an exaggerated confidence in mechanisms instead of freedom,
with an accompanying forgetfulness of the risks of freedom and of
the possibility that man, on the very day after the revolution, might
still do wrong, reestablish a system built on domination, and surren-
der to corruption.

Father Arrupe certainly wanted to be correctly understood; he
stated clearly that he was obliged to fight with equal vigor

> the efforts of anyone who wishes to take advantage of our reserva-
> tions about marxist analysis in order to condemn as marxist or
> communist, or at least to minimize esteem for, a commitment to
> justice and the cause of the poor, the defence of their rights against
> those who exploit them, the urging of legitimate claims. Have we
> not often seen forms of anticommunism that are nothing but means
> for concealing injustice? (345)

On the other hand, Marxism is not alone in resting on "surrepti-
tiously introduced" presuppositions which demand the critical attention of Christians, including Jesuits.

> In particular, the type of social analysis used in the liberal world
> today implies an individualistic and materialistic vision of life that

is destructive of christian values and attitudes. In this connection, are we giving enough attention to the content of textbooks used in our schools? (344)

## Participation in the Transformation of Structures

The letter on Marxist social analysis represented an important stage in the interpretation and use of Decree 4. Indirectly it touched on another difficult problem, that of seeing how religious and priests, specifically Jesuits, could and should make a contribution to the effort to transform structures. A vexing question indeed, for there was much disagreement among Jesuits and in wider circles about the structures in question. Institutions, undoubtedly, but also much broader systems, including mental structures or ways of doing and thinking. Similarly, public opinion or the atmosphere which takes shape and establishes itself, so that apart from it one can hardly function. Finally, we include the equally complex question of how to attack structures or to transform them.

In general, when we speak about "structures," we have in mind any established situation which, as long as it remains unchanged, renders it impossible for people both individually and collectively to establish right order where disorder prevails, and this despite their good will. Conversely, there are also helpful social structures. In Decree 4 "structure" refers to realities or forces which go beyond human strength or at least the strength of the individual. They are "among the principal formative influences in our world, shaping people's ideas and feelings, shaping their most intimate desires and aspirations" (no. 40 [89]).

Involved here are realities which are not entirely clear, which loom over humankind. At the same time, however, Decree 4 observes that they are better understood today, that at least their "mechanisms and laws" are being discovered (no. 31 [80]). This knowledge makes action on them possible, something that was hardly ever the case before. Given this possibility, "service according to the Gospel cannot dispense with a carefully planned effort to exert influence on those [social, economic, and political] structures" (no. 31 [80]).

Some of the most trustworthy criteria provided to guide Jesuits in the choices they make of ministries recommend work designed to change structures. The members of the general congregation made this clear before posing questions to themselves:

> For the greater glory of God and salvation of men, Ignatius desired that his companions go wherever there was hope of the more universal good; go to those who have been abandoned; go to those who are in greatest need. But where is the greatest need today? Where are we to locate this hope for the more universal good? (D. 4, no. 39 [88])

The response to the questions brings us back to social structures and the work needed to transform them "in the interest of the spiritual and material liberation of fellow human beings" (no. 40 [89]). Clearly, there is no affirmation here that such work is equivalently the service that Jesuits, in accord with their vocation, should provide for achieving a more universal good. The congregation affirms only that the transformation of structures "is intimately connected to the work of evangelization" (no. 40 [89]). This section of Decree 4 concludes as follows:

> From this point of view, . . . desire for the more universal good is perfectly compatible with the determination to serve the most afflicted for the sake of the Gospel. Our preaching will be heard to the extent that witness accompanies it, the witness of commitment to the promotion of justice as an anticipation of the Kingdom which is to come. (no. 41 [90])

Assuredly there are many different ways of acting on structures, depending on what kind they are. Not every kind of action is equally appropriate for priests and religious. In general, no single action brings about the transformation of structures or institutions; usually a series of initiatives is required to achieve this.

Nor is structural transformation always brought about by direct political action. For example, assisting poor people, helping them to build new production cooperatives or to organize their environment or housing, has been effective, as have forms of assistance enabling them to develop community or take charge of their own destiny. These are forms of action where religious or priests have been able to be very effective.

Action directed toward changing institutions can also be carried on through efforts to form public opinion concerning them. Bear in mind, though, that public opinion is itself a structure open to transformation. Such efforts, generally speaking, are one form of action in harmony with the mission of an apostolic group like the Society of Jesus provided that the values in the name of which reforms are promoted are carefully spelled out, and that the concrete steps toward this end rely more on lay competence and political forces than on the efforts of priests or religious.

One might think, on the other hand, that there is a great gulf between the transformation of structures and the apostolate of education. On the contrary, the truth is that education can be a powerful lever directed toward changing ways of thinking, even an entire mental climate—certain structures, therefore—always provided that the education in question is energetically pointed toward the promotion of justice. Father Arrupe, for example, never wearied of calling for education of that kind, as can be seen in his 1980 summons to secondary schools to form new "men and women for service" according to the Gospel. He went on to say:

> If the finality of our education is the creation of new persons, men and women of service, then what are the **pedagogical** repercussions? . . . A desire for Christian witness, service of one another, cannot thrive in an atmosphere of academic competition, or where one's personal qualities are judged only by comparison to those of others. These things will thrive only in an atmosphere in which we learn how to be available, how to be of service to others. [We need to form] the evangelical person, who looks on every other man and woman as a brother or sister.[3]

Moreover, whatever may have been said, there is no doubt about Decree 4's affirmation of the importance of education, an apostolate to be "intensified" and thoroughly renewed "in every sphere." Such renewal "will contribute to the formation of those who by a kind of multiplier effect will share in the process of educating the world itself" (no. 60 [109]).

---

[3] Final address to a symposium on secondary education, delivered on September 13, 1980 (*Acta Romana* 18, no. 1 [1980]: 263).

In what concerns structured ways of collective thinking, Decree 4 looked to the work realizable by the communication media. In this Jesuits can "only help to the extent that we succeed in humanizing the social climate—attitudes and behavior—where we are engaged" (no. 60 [109]).

## Always Finding the Right Way for Acting to Transform Structures

A fundamental consideration for Jesuits regarding action directed to transforming structures, whether they are institutions or mind-sets, is that they always balance it against more direct activity to help people toward conversion of heart and discernment of God's will. Decree 4, then, does not recommend blind or exclusive confidence in such actions as a means of the apostolate, as the following makes clear:

> [S]ervice according to the Gospel cannot dispense with a carefully planned effort to exert influence on those structures.
>
> We must bear in mind, however, that our efforts to promote justice and human freedom on the social and structural level, necessary though they are, are not sufficient of themselves. Injustice must be attacked at its roots which are in the human heart by transforming those attitudes and habits which beget injustice and foster the structures of oppression. (no. 31f [80f])

Effective apostolic work includes very personal approaches to people, as well as those more general means (education and mass media) which we have just considered. These more general approaches lead to changes in the social atmosphere, public opinion, and mindsets.

A bit further on in Decree 4, we read:

> This is not to say, of course, that we can ever afford to neglect the direct apostolate to individuals, to those who are the victims of the injustice of social structures as well as to those who bear some responsibility or influence over them. (no. 40 [89])

To work along these two lines at the same time is certainly never easy; but it is as unavoidable an obligation as that of working simultaneously for the service of the faith and the promotion of justice. In this regard we are fully aware that, demanded though the latter is by the faith-commitment, it is only a part and never the whole. It is an obligation similar to the perennial Jesuit responsibility to seek the conversion of those in high position who can wield much influence, while at the same time never neglecting to teach Christ's way to children and simple, ordinary people. This is the powerful ideal of St. Ignatius, who always drew inspiration from a maxim like the following, which summarizes his way of describing the Christian paradox: "Not to be limited by what is greatest, yet to be contained by what is smallest—that is divine."

### Political Implications

In what concerns political involvement, the following summary of the decision of former general congregations expresses the tradition of the Society up to the year 1974. Jesuits should refrain from taking part in the handling of political matters and even, so far as is possible, avoid giving occasion for even ill-founded suspicion of their involvement. This prohibition, however, does not apply to efforts directed to having the principles of Christianity penetrate public life, provided that the means used to this end are in conformity with our Institute.[4]

General Congregation 32 did not change the central core of this tradition. It did, however, take it up in a somewhat different way. The congregation, first of all, had to emphasize that the option to promote justice as an integral part of Jesuit service of the faith could not avoid having effects on the political level. "Any realistic plan to engage in the promotion of justice will mean some kind of involvement in civic activity" (D. 4, no. 80 [129]). "Civic" meant "political" in this context, as members of the congregation remembered. Other expressions underlined the necessity of being open to new forms of action. Thus, after Decree 4 had treated social analysis and "pastoral and apostolic discernment" of situations, we read the following: "From analysis and discernment will come committed action; from the experience of action will come insight into how to proceed further" (no. 44 [93]).

---

[4] See, for example, *Societatis Iesu Constitutiones et Epitome Instituti* (Rome, General Curia of the Society of Jesus, 1962), no. 682, §2, and no. 700, §2.

Immediately thereafter, are these lines: "The superior will enable the members of the community not only to understand and appreciate the particular—and possibly unusual—apostolates undertaken by their companions under obedience, but also to take joint responsibility for them" (no. 45 [94]). Even if suffering is involved as a result. So here we have an invitation to much bolder activities than we would spontaneously accept.

Having said this, the congregation did not neglect to reaffirm the explicit ban on exercising political authority or playing a role in political parties, in conformity with the Society's tradition. "Exceptional forms of involvement must conform to the general practice of the Church and the norms laid down by Father General," Decree 4 makes clear, referring in a footnote to the 1971 synod of bishops (no. 80 [129]). Actually, Father General expressly reserved to himself the power to give permission to Jesuits to stand for elective political offices.[5]

In its discussion of the responsibility of others "in the social order" to advance solidarity with those without voice or power, the congregation spoke clearly about "our own responsibilities" (D. 4, no. 42 [91]). A bit further on, speaking of sharing in efforts to promote justice, it specified that Jesuits were to do so "in our own particular way without seeking to implicate or compete with [other groups'] strengths" (no. 43 [92]). In his letter of May 2, 1975, Cardinal Villot, speaking in the name of Pope Paul VI, did not contradict these statements in any way, but certainly did clarify them by insisting on the necessity of not forgetting "that the priest should inspire lay Catholics, since in the promotion of justice theirs is the more demanding role. The tasks proper to each should not be confused."[6]

---

[5] "If, in certain countries, it seems necessary to adopt more detailed norms and directives, this must be seen to by provincials—as far as possible in regional conferences. These norms and directives should be submitted to Father General for approval. It will then be for the provincial—with the agreement, where the case demands it, of the local bishop or the bishops' conference—to give or refuse the permission that may be required" (no. 80 [129]).

[6] May 2, 1975, letter of the Cardinal Secretary of State to Father General, *Documents,* 548.

Certainly, in practice some problems arose in the Society regarding political involvement, on more than one occasion calling for clarification. Father Arrupe took up the matter in the 1978 congregation of procurators. He did not hesitate to use the term "political engagement" in referring to certain consequences of Jesuit work in the struggle for justice and solidarity with the poor. "Up to a certain point, the struggle for justice and solidarity with the poor are inevitably linked with political engagement." He continued by pointing out that if the principles governing Jesuit apostolic work and the totality of the orientations found in Decree 4 are not clear, "some aberrations can result and in fact have resulted." For this reason, he continued, provincials of various countries and he himself "have had to clarify some concrete cases involving positive political action of a partisan nature or the acceptance of positions or responsibilities in ideological and political movements of one or other type that are incompatible with our mission."[7]

Both John Paul I during his brief pontificate and then John Paul II insisted on the concreteness of situations and of the mission of priests and religious in the political domain. Father Paolo Dezza, the pontifical delegate who replaced Father Arrupe, more than once provided explanations in the name of John Paul II, spelling out the role of inspiration, guidance, and teaching proper to priests, adding the following in very clear terms: "Ours cannot take part in political parties or assume directly political positions, save in really exceptional cases, approved by the Bishops and by Father General."[8]

In the meantime, Father Robert Drinan, on orders from the Pope, withdrew as a candidate for reelection to the U.S. House of Representatives, and other Jesuits were ordered to give up political functions they were exercising or to withdraw from political parties to which they belonged. All in all, very few men were involved.

In 1983 General Congregation 33 acknowledged that not all Jesuits in years past had always carefully assessed the role proper to them, quite different from the role proper to the laity, in what

---

[7] *Acta Romana* 17, no. 2 (1978): 456.

[8] Letter of Father Dezza to the whole Society following the meeting of provincials (*Acta Romana* 18 [1982]: 793).

concerned actions for the transformation of structures, most especially in political matters. Consequently, it stressed with new vigor all the directives we have just considered. On the other hand, it did not fail to encourage Jesuits to involve themselves in promoting justice through activity which might have incidental political aspects. "As an international body, the Society of Jesus commits itself to that work which is the promotion of a more just world order, greater solidarity of rich countries with poor, and a lasting peace based on human rights and freedom (GC 33, D. 1, no 46 [49]). Again, an invitation to work on behalf of peace.

The congregation went on to list for Jesuits a whole series of questions calling for their attention, such as the following:

- Attacks by governments on human rights through assassination, imprisonment, torture, the denial of religious freedom and political expression: all of which cause so many to suffer, some of them fellow Jesuits

- the sad plight of millions of refugees searching for a permanent home, a situation brought to our special attention by Father Arrupe

- discrimination against whole categories of human beings, such as migrants and racial or religious minorities

- the unjust treatment and exploitation of women

- public policies and social attitudes which threaten human life for the unborn, the handicapped and the aged

- economic oppression and spiritual needs of the unemployed, of poor and landless peasants, and of workers, with whom many Jesuits, like our worker priests, have identified themselves in order to bring them the Good News. (no. 45 [48])

So the invitation was always there to undertake apostolic work capable of influencing solutions to the most burning social and political questions; however, this invitation certainly excluded political authority and political activities which normally belong to the laity. The 1971 synod of bishops dwelt upon this fundamental distinction with extraordinary persistence. Its explanation referred both to the primordial functions of unity entrusted to priests and shared by religious, as well as the need for them to devote themselves primarily to spiritual ministries where nobody else could replace them.

Now that we understand these functions and tasks more clearly than ever before because of what has been said above, we should at the same time learn not to be upset by the "political" repercussions or implications of activity favoring the promotion of justice. This includes the work of encouraging lay men and women to play their part; it embraces also education and pastoral denunciations of injustices. Such work definitely forms part of the ministry of both Jesuits and other priests. Decree 4 invited Jesuits to interior freedom and courage in this regard, an invitation not to be forgotten. This kind of spiritual freedom will certainly make us more effective than we could hope to be if we took on directly combative functions or public responsibilities. Clear speech is needed, but speech appropriate to one's place.

Since in the practical order differences in such matters will never be lacking and will clearly have very practical aspects, the importance both of communal discernment, the results of which are to be submitted to superiors, and of fidelity to the local ecclesiastical hierarchy has been stressed more than once in recent years. This is still a guideline to follow. Nor should we forget the statement of Paul VI transmitted to the Jesuits in 1975: "Work for the promotion of justice should be undertaken in accord with directives drawn up by the local hierarchy and in consideration of the conditions peculiar to each region."[9] Naturally, there is no way to avoid situations where the local hierarchy is not entirely in agreement on a matter. The directive of Paul VI also describes the spirit in which one should act in such a situation.

At the end of its discussions about Decree 4 and its application, General Congregation 33 returned to this point. Thus, for example, it said: "[L]et the entire Society seek to incorporate itself more and more vigorously and creatively **in the life of the Church** so that we may experience and live its mystery within ourselves" (D. 1, no. 8 [8], emphasis added). Again, it recalled the spirit of the Council: "The full realization of the Church's missions after the Second Vatican Council calls us to sincere collaboration with the bishops, with other religious, with the diocesan clergy, and with other Christians as well as with people of other religious faiths" (no. 47

---

[9] *Documents*, 548.

[50]). In this array we are especially mindful of bishops and the local church. The recommendation itself is valid for all the fields of apostolic work, but it is particularly applicable to any field of activity involving some political aspect, such as we have just considered.

In what concerns the Society of Jesus, General Congregation 33 declared the following:

> Our experiences of recent years have made us increasingly aware that the more a priest is exposed to situations and structures alien to the faith, the more he must strengthen his own religious identity and his union with the whole body of the Society as represented by the local community to which he belongs. (no. 33 [36)

By implication, what was said about the local community applies to the local church as well.

Returning for the last time to the basic position of Decree 4 on the political implications of apostolic action which involves the promotion of justice as an essential necessity, we can say that it has exorcised a frequently found type of timidity. It does so by making us see as something quite natural "activities on the social and collective plane flowing from the apostolate." It insists, on the other hand, that we should not give in to the temptation to have recourse to political tactics or even to directly political influence sought for itself. All of these points have been clearly stated, not weakened, by both papal statements and General Congregation 33 itself. Quite probably with the passage of time we will learn and understand still more clearly and precisely how courage or frank statements are to be combined with perfect freedom regarding organized political forces or public functions, as recommended here. Involvement is called for, always with the understanding that it is to be pure service of faith and of the message of salvation, free of all contamination by special interests or ideologies.

# Conclusion

A dopting Decree 4, *Service of Faith and the Promotion of Justice,* caused the Society of Jesus to pass through an important stage, as did the ensuing developments and events, including the clarification which the Holy See felt obliged to insist upon to assure its correct application. Our presumption has been that an account of this history can be enlightening also to non-Jesuits.

In conclusion, it is fitting to underline clearly that Jesuits were not alone in enacting and then trying to carry into practice resolutions in favor of the promotion of justice and the like. Different groups of bishops have been active in various parts of the world. In addition to the Latin American bishops at Puebla, we have recalled the 1974 pastoral session of French bishops on "Human Liberation and Salvation in Jesus Christ," as well as the meeting of Italian bishops in 1976 dealing with the theme "Evangelization and Human Promotion." At this point we would like to insist a bit more on the role of a sizable number of religious congregations who quite explicitly committed themselves to the same course.

Often enough the dominant theme of their resolutions was the preferential option for the poor. As one example we might cite what the Carmelites did in their 1980 general chapter held in Rio de Janeiro. We should not overlook the fact, however, that the option for the poor also included an awareness of and concern about injustices. The declaration of the Carmelite chapter, "Called to Give an Account to the Poor," specifically mentioned "the economic and political dependence preventing a fair distribution of this world's goods," as well as the entire "system" which in the Latin American context "militated against human well-being." The preferential option for the poor was also described as an option in favor of "the underprivileged" or "the little ones." The declaration was quite clear that

> Our choice is not without risk of being misunderstood or excluded, losing acquired positions, or being crushed by the powerful of this world. . . . We should seriously look upon our lives as being a sort of martyrdom and we should set about walking the way of the cross of the little ones of our world.[1]

In 1982 the Society of the Divine Word (S.V.D.) in its turn published a document explicitly entitled "Promotion of Justice and Peace, in Oneness with the Poor." The Dominicans linked justice and peace in a statement of their 1983 general chapter. They specified **three** options: for the poor, for justice, for peace. We can see how the concerns converged. Other examples could be cited from religious congregations of both women and men. The Dominicans had previously given priority to "social justice," but their new document stated the following: "Many brethren consider such questions as topics reserved for specialists."[2] Looking to the future the new document states the following:

> Our option for justice and the poor demands a denunciation of unjust structures and a struggle to establish fraternity and reconciliation for the world and an effort toward our own conversion. Not to opt for the poor is to fall into the danger of making an option for the rich.
>
> It is necessary also to point out prudently the mutual dependence existing between poverty, the violation of human rights, systematic exploitation of the arms race and international financial organizations. (no. [34] B)

Let us likewise note the formula of the Society of the Divine Word, which recalls Decree 4 of the Jesuits: "Our own participation in the mission of the Church as a religious missionary society also

---

[1] [Translator's note: This quotation is taken from an unpublished private document available to the author.]

[2] *Acts of the Elective General Chapter of the Orders of Friars Preachers,* 1983, c. 14, no. [34] A.

involves 'action on behalf of justice and participation in the transformation of the world.'"[3]

In the chapter on concrete proposals, we find in the first place a call for "conscientization and insertion into the life of the poor." This statement then follows:

> Only a constant process of conscientization and a critical analysis of the socio-political situation in which we live and work can open our eyes to the plight of the poor and oppressed. Therefore we should make use of every opportunity to share more closely, at least for a time, the misery, insecurity and frustration that is the lot of so many today (7).

On the other hand, we read: "Our response . . . calls us to engage more directly in apostolates for and with the poor."

There then follows a list of such options:

- relief services directed towards immediately ameliorating abject conditions of poverty brought about by natural calamities or social upheavals
- social projects aimed at helping the poor . . . [through] dispensaries, orphanages, etc.
- development programs directed towards organizing the poor into selfreliant communities . . .
- conscientization or the process of awakening the poor to their own needs and potentialities, accompanying them in their struggle for equality and participation in the decision making processes . . .
- speaking out publicly against actual cases of human rights violations and abuse of power
- participation in and support of peace movements. . . . (8)

Then there follow some clarifications similar to those we have already listed. We note in particular:

> Our commitment to the promotion of justice and peace should never be a function of any ideology but flow from Jesus' own predilection for the poor and maginalized. . . .

---

[3] General Chapter of the Society of the Divine Word, *The Promotion of Justice and Peace in Solidarity with the Poor in the Light of Constitution 112 II Directives on Poverty and Finances* (January 1983), p. 3.

Solidarity with the poor in the light of the kingdom demands a spirituality deeply aware that the human liberation we seek is not only a task but also a gift. . . . If it were only a task, our involvement could easily lead to bitterness, cynicism and despair. But since it is also a gift, we can then persevere in faith and hope. Understanding that God's kingdom is already operative in the present enables us to radiate joy in the midst of situations which humanly speaking may appear utterly hopeless.

It is impossible not to be impressed by the generosity and scope of these resolutions and programs. The element which perhaps was specifically true of the Jesuits is that circumstances led them to develop a series of reflections on the theological foundations of the relation of justice to the Gospel, of justice to charity, of love of neighbor to love of God, of faith to justice itself. They were likewise led to probe very carefully problems such as social analysis, the appropriate forms of participation by religious and priests in activities directed toward structural transformation, and the political implications of commitment to the cause of justice. All of these practical problems followed in the wake of the options taken for the promotion of justice. However, all this is but a small contribution to a structure that has only begun to take shape. For it looks as though this whole set of questions, bearing the stamp of the Second Vatican Council, will not disappear so soon from the conscience of the Church, especially from the consciences of those of its members who more fully devote themselves to the work of evangelizing.

In the first stages of this task of promoting justice as a requisite for the service of faith, mistakes, some of them serious, were made. Here and there these errors led at times to forgetfulness of faith itself and its centrality. But none of these defects could prevent the demand for a concrete link between justice and faith from enduring. That link is based on the compelling reevaluation of "human activity in the universe" which distinguished Vatican II, especially *Gaudium et spes*. The council opened our eyes again to the teaching on the importance for eternity which in virtue of the grace of Christ can be present in the works of time. From this point of view, the very work of evangelization inescapably calls for the participation of men and women in the task of human development and the promotion of justice.

Thus, an entirely new way of life has begun to take shape among Jesuits and many others. This new way of looking at life and of living is not the only channel through which the Gospel reaches us today. But it is one of them, a quite decisive one, at a time when men and women are attracted as never before to the very task of building the human person. Surely we are obliged to help all to advance that endeavor involving the very work of Christ and the glory of God.

# DECREE FOUR

## *OUR MISSION TODAY: THE SERVICE OF FAITH AND THE PROMOTION OF JUSTICE*

## Introduction and Summary

1.  To the many requests received from all parts of the Society for clear decisions and definite guidelines concerning our mission today, the 32nd General Congregation responds as follows.

2.  The mission of the Society of Jesus today is the service of faith, of which the promotion of justice is an absolute requirement. For reconciliation with God demands the reconciliation of people with one another.

3.  In one form or another, this has always been the mission of the Society;[1] but it gains new meaning and urgency in the light of the needs and aspirations of the men and women of our time, and it is in that light that we examine it anew. We are confronted today, in fact, by a whole series of new challenges.

4.  There is a new challenge to our apostolic mission in a fact without precedent in the history of mankind: today, more than two billion human beings have no knowledge of God the Father and His Son, Jesus Christ, whom He has sent,[2] yet feel an increasing hunger for the God they already adore in the depths of their hearts without knowing Him explicitly.

5.  There is a new challenge to our apostolic mission in that many of our contemporaries, dazzled and even dominated by the achievements of the human mind, forgetting or rejecting the mystery of man's ultimate meaning, have thus lost the sense of God.

6.  There is a new challenge to our apostolic mission in a world increasingly interdependent but, for all that, divided by injustice: injustice not only personal but institutionalized: built into economic, social, and political structures that dominate the life of nations and the international community.

---

[1] See *FI*, especially [3] (1). The Formula was approved by Popes Paul III and Julius III.

[2] See *SpEx*, 102.

7.  Our response to these new challenges will be unavailing unless it is total, corporate, rooted in faith and experience, and multiform.

•  **total:** While relying on prayer, and acting on the conviction that God alone can change the human heart, we must throw into this enterprise all that we are and have, our whole persons, our communities, institutions, ministries, resources.

•  **corporate:** Each one of us must contribute to the total mission according to his talents and functions which, in collaboration with the efforts of others, give life to the whole body. This collaborative mission is exercised under the leadership of Peter's Successor who presides over the universal Church and over all those whom the Spirit of God has appointed Pastors over the churches.[3]

•  **rooted in faith and experience:** It is from faith and experience combined that we will learn how to respond most appropriately to new needs arising from new situations.

•  **multiform:** Since these situations are different in different parts of the world, we must cultivate a great adaptability and flexibility within the single, steady aim of the service of faith and the promotion of justice.

8.  While offering new challenges to our apostolic mission, the modern world provides new tools as well: new and more effective ways of understanding man, nature and society; of communicating thought, image and feeling; of organizing action. These we must learn to use in the service of evangelization and human development.

9.  Consequently we must undertake a thoroughgoing reassessment of our traditional apostolic methods, attitudes and institutions with a view to adapting them to the new needs of the times and to a world in process of rapid change.

10.  All this demands that we practice discernment, that spiritual discernment which St. Ignatius teaches us in the Exercises. Moreover discernment will yield a deeper grasp of the movements,

---

[3] See LG, 22.

aspirations and struggles in the hearts of our contemporaries, as well as those in the heart of mankind itself.

11. In short, our mission today is to preach Jesus Christ and to make Him known in such a way that all men and women are able to recognize Him whose delight, from the beginning, has been to be with the sons of men and to take an active part in their history.[4]

12. In carrying out this mission, we should be convinced, today more than ever, that "the means which unite the human instrument with God and so dispose it that it may be wielded dexterously by His divine hand are more effective than those which equip it in relation to men."[5]

✤     *Section A*

## OUR MISSION YESTERDAY AND TODAY

### *The Charism of the Society*

13. The mission we are called to share is the mission of the Church itself, to make known to men and women the love of God our Father, a love whose promise is eternal life. It is from the loving regard of God upon the world that the mission of Jesus takes its rise, Jesus who was sent "not to be served but to serve, and to give His life as a ransom for many."[6] The mission of Christ, in turn, gives rise to the mission shared by all Christians as members of the Church sent to bring all men and women the Good News of their salvation and that "they may have life and have it to the full."[7]

14. St. Ignatius and his first companions, in the spiritual experience of the Exercises, were moved to a searching consideration of

---

[4] See Prov. 8: 22–31; Col. 1:15–20.

[5] *Cons.* [13].

[6] Matt. 20:28.

[7] John 10:10. See Matt. 9:36, 10:1–42; John 6.

the world of their own time in order to discover its needs. They contemplated "how the Three Divine Persons look down upon the whole expanse or circuit of all the earth, filled with human beings" and decide "that the Second Person should become man to save the human race." Then they turned their eyes to where God's gaze was fixed, and saw for themselves the men and women of their time, one after another, "with such great diversity in dress and in manners of acting. Some are white, some black; some at peace, and some at war; some weeping, some laughing; some well, some sick; some coming into the world, some dying, etc."[8] That was how they learned to respond to the call of Christ and to work for the establishment of His Kingdom.[9]

15.   United in a single vision of faith, strong in a common hope and rooted in the same love of Christ whose companions they wished to be, Ignatius and his first band of apostles believed that the service they could give to the people of their time would be more effective if they were more closely bound to one another as members of a single body, at once religious, apostolic and priestly, and united to the Successor of Peter by a special bond of love and service reflecting their total availability for mission in the universal Church.

16.   It is in this light that we are asked to renew our dedication to the properly apostolic dimension of our religious life. Our consecration to God is really a prophetic rejection of those idols which the world is always tempted to adore, wealth, pleasure, prestige, power. Hence our poverty, chastity and obedience ought visibly to bear witness to this. Despite the inadequacy of any attempt to anticipate the Kingdom which is to come, our vows ought to show how by God's grace there can be, as the Gospel proclaims, a community among human beings which is based on sharing rather than on greed; on willing openness to all persons rather than on seeking after the privileges of caste or class or race; on service rather than on domination and exploitation. The men and women of our time need a hope which is eschatological, but they also need to have some signs that its realization has already begun.

---

[8] *SpEx*, 102, 106 (Contemplation on the Incarnation).

[9] Ibid., 91–100 (Contemplation of the "Kingdom").

17. Finally, the Apostolic Letters of Paul III (1540) and Julius III (1550) recognize that the Society of Jesus was founded "chiefly for this purpose: to strive especially for the defense and propagation of the faith, and for the progress of souls in Christian life and doctrine, by means of public preaching, lectures, and any other ministrations whatsoever of the word of God, and further, by means of the Spiritual Exercises, the education of children and unlettered persons in Christianity, and the spiritual consolation of Christ's faithful through hearing confessions and administering the other sacraments," as well as "in reconciling the estranged, in holily assisting and serving those who are found in prisons and hospitals, and indeed in performing any other works of charity, according to what will seem expedient for the glory of God and the common good."[10] This primordial statement remains for us a normative one.

18. The mission of the Society today is the priestly service of the faith, an apostolate whose aim is to help people become more open toward God and more willing to live according to the demands of the Gospel. The Gospel demands a life freed from egoism and self-seeking, from all attempts to seek one's own advantage and from every form of exploitation of one's neighbor. It demands a life in which the justice of the Gospel shines out in a willingness not only to recognize and respect the rights of all, especially the poor and the powerless, but also to work actively to secure those rights. It demands an openness and generosity to anyone in need, even a stranger or an enemy. It demands towards those who have injured us, pardon; toward those with whom we are at odds, a spirit of reconciliation. We do not acquire this attitude of mind by our own efforts alone. It is the fruit of the Spirit who transforms our hearts and fills them with the power of God's mercy, that mercy whereby he most fully shows forth His justice by drawing us, unjust though we are, to His friendship.[11] It is by this that we know that the promotion of justice is an integral part of the priestly service of the faith.

---

[10] *FI*, [3] (1), approved by Julius III.

[11] See Rom. 5:89.

19. In his address of December 3, 1974,[12] Pope Paul VI confirmed "as a modern expression of your vow of obedience to the Pope" that we offer resistance to the many forms of contemporary atheism. This was the mission he entrusted to us at the time of the 31st General Congregation, and in recalling it he commended the way in which the Society down the years has been present at the heart of ideological battles and social conflicts, wherever the crying needs of mankind encountered the perennial message of the Gospel. Thus if we wish to continue to be faithful to this special character of our vocation and to the mission we have received from the Pope, we must "contemplate" our world as Ignatius did his, that we may hear anew the call of Christ dying and rising in the anguish and aspirations of men and women.

20. There are millions of men and women in our world, specific people with names and faces, who are suffering from poverty and hunger, from the unjust distribution of wealth and resources and from the consequences of racial, social, and political discrimination. Not only the quality of life but human life itself is under constant threat. It is becoming more and more clear that despite the opportunities offered by an ever more serviceable technology, we are simply not willing to pay the price of a more just and more humane society.[13]

21. At the same time, people today are somehow aware that their problems are not just social and technological, but personal and spiritual. They have a feeling that what is at stake here is the very meaning of man: his future and his destiny. People are hungry: hungry not just for bread, but for the Word of God (Deut. 8:3; Matt. 4:4). For this reason the Gospel should be preached with a fresh vigor, for it is in a position once again to make itself heard. At first sight God might seem to have no place in public life, nor even in

---

[12] Pope Paul VI, "Address to the Members of the 32nd General Congregation," December 3, 1974, pp. 519–536.

[13] We find a Gospel echo, a truly apostolic echo of the anguish and questioning of our times, in *Gaudium et Spes, Mater et Magistra, Pacem in Terris, Populorum Progressio, Octogesima Adveniens*. In these documents of the church's magisterium the needs of our world touch us and break in upon us both on the level of our personal lives and of our apostolic service.

private awareness. Yet everywhere, if we only know how to look, we can see that people are groping towards an experience of Christ and waiting in hope for His Kingdom of love, of justice and of peace.

22. Of these expectations and converging desires the last two Synods of Bishops have reminded us in their reflections on *Justice in the World* and *Evangelization in the Modern World.* They point to concrete forms which our witness and our mission must take today.

23. The expectations of our contemporaries—and their problems —are ours as well. We ourselves share in the blindness and injustice of our age. We ourselves stand in need of being evangelized. We ourselves need to know how to meet Christ as He works in the world through the power of His Spirit. And it is to this world, our world, that we are sent. Its needs and aspirations are an appeal to the Gospel which it is our mission to proclaim.

❖ *Section B*

## THE CHALLENGES WE FACE

### New Demands, New Hopes

24. The first thing that must be said about the world which it is our mission to evangelize is this: everywhere, but in very different situations, we have to preach Jesus Christ to men and women who have never really heard of Him, or who do not yet know of Him sufficiently.

a) In what were once called "mission lands" our predecessors endeavored by their preaching of the Gospel to set up and foster new Christian communities. This task of direct evangelization by the preaching of Jesus Christ remains essential today, and must be continued, since never before have there been so many people who have never heard the Word of Christ the Savior. At the same time dialog with the believers of other religions is becoming for us an ever more important apostolate.

b) In the traditionally Christian countries, the works we established, the movements we fostered, the institutions—retreat houses, schools, universities—we set up, are still necessary for the service of faith. But there are many in these countries who can no longer be reached by the ministries exercised through these works and institutions. The so-called "Christian" countries have themselves become "mission lands."

25. The second decisive factor for our preaching of Jesus Christ and his Gospel is this: the new opportunities—and problems—disclosed in our time by the discoveries of technology and the human sciences. They have introduced a relativism, often of a very radical kind, into the picture of man and the world to which we were accustomed, with the result that traditional perspectives have altered almost beyond recognition. Changes of this kind in the mind-sets and structures of society inevitably produce strong repercussions in our lives as individuals and as members of society. As a result, there has been gradual erosion of traditional values, and gradual diminution of reliance on the power of traditional symbols. Simultaneously, new aspirations arise which seek to express themselves in the planning and implementation of practical programs.

26. The secularization of man and the world takes different forms in different groups, classes, ages and parts of the world, and in all its forms offers challenges to the preaching of the Gospel to which there is no ready-made answer.

a) On the one hand, certain false images of God which prop up and give an aura of legitimacy to unjust social structures are no longer acceptable. Neither can we admit those more ambiguous images of God which appear to release man from his inalienable responsibilities. We feel this just as much as our contemporaries do; even more, perhaps, given our commitment to proclaim the God who has revealed himself in Christ. For our own sake, just as much as for the sake of our contemporaries, we must find a new language, a new set of symbols, that will enable us to leave our fallen idols behind us and rediscover the true God: the God who, in Jesus Christ, chose to share our human pilgrimage and make our human destiny irrevocably his own. To live our lives "in memory of Him" requires of us this creative effort of faith.

b) On the other hand, part of the framework within which we have preached the Gospel is now perceived as being inextricably linked to an unacceptable social order, and for that reason is being called into question. Our apostolic institutions, along with many of those of the Church herself, are involved in the same crisis that social institutions in general are presently undergoing. Here again is an experience we share with our contemporaries, and in a particularly painful way. The relevance of our work as religious, priests and apostles is often enough not evident to the men and women around us. Not only that; despite the firmness of our faith and our convictions the relevance of what we do may not be clear, sometimes, even to ourselves. This unsettles us, and in our insecurity we tend to respond to questioning with silence and to shy away from confrontation. Yet there are signs of a contemporary religious revival which should encourage us to reaffirm our commitment with courage, and not only to welcome but to seek new opportunities for evangelization.

27. Finally, a third characteristic of our world particularly significant to our mission of evangelization is this: it is now within human power to make the world more just—but we do not really want to. Our new mastery over nature and man himself is used, often enough, to exploit individuals, groups and peoples rather than to distribute the resources of the planet more equitably. It has led, it is leading, to division rather than union, to alienation rather than communication, to oppression and domination rather than to a greater respect for the rights of individuals or of groups, and a more real brotherhood among men. We can no longer pretend that the inequalities and injustices of our world must be borne as part of the inevitable order of things. It is now quite apparent that they are the result of what man himself, man in his selfishness, has done. Hence there can be no promotion of justice in the full and Christian sense unless we also preach Jesus Christ and the mystery of reconciliation He brings. It is Christ who, in the last analysis, opens the way to the complete and definitive liberation of mankind for which we long from the bottom of our hearts. Conversely, it will not be possible to bring Christ to people or to proclaim His Gospel effectively unless a firm decision is taken to devote ourselves to the promotion of justice.

28. From all over the world where Jesuits are working, very similar and very insistent requests have been made that, by a clear decision on the part of the General Congregation, the Society should commit itself to work for the promotion of justice. Our apostolate today urgently requires that we take this decision. As apostles we are bearers of the Christian message. And at the heart of the Christian message is God revealing Himself in Christ as the Father of us all whom through the Spirit He calls to conversion. In its integrity, then, conversion means accepting that we are at one and the same time children of the Father and brothers and sisters of each other. There is no genuine conversion to the love of God without conversion to the love of neighbor and, therefore, to the demands of justice. Hence, fidelity to our apostolic mission requires that we propose the whole of Christian salvation and lead others to embrace it. Christian salvation consists in an undivided love of the Father and of the neighbor and of justice. Since evangelization is proclamation of that faith which is made operative in love of others,[14] the promotion of justice is indispensable to it.

29. What is at stake here is the fruitfulness of all our apostolic endeavors, and notably of any coherent attempt to combat atheism. The injustice that racks our world in so many forms is, in fact, a denial of God in practice, for it denies the dignity of the human person, the image of God, the brother or sister of Christ.[15] The cult of money, progress, prestige and power has as its fruit the sin of institutionalized injustice condemned by the Synod of 1971, and it leads to the enslavement not only of the oppressed, but of the oppressor as well—and to death.

30. At a time when so many people are sparing no effort to put the world to rights without reference to God, our endeavor should be to show as clearly as we can that our Christian hope is not a dull opiate, but a firm and realistic commitment to make our world other than it is, to make it the visible sign of another world, the sign—and

---

[14] See Gal. 5:6; Eph. 4:15.

[15] On the dignity of man, image of God and brother of Christ see: LG, 42; GS, 22, 24, 29, 38, 93; *Nuntium Concilii Vaticani II ad omnes homines,* December 20, 1962; Declarations of the Synods of Bishops of 1971, 1974; Addresses of Pope Paul VI.

pledge—of "a new heaven and a new earth."[16] The last Synod vigorously recalled this for us: "The Gospel entrusted to us is the good news of salvation for man and the whole of society, which must begin here and now to manifest itself on earth even if mankind's liberation in all its fullness will be achieved only beyond the frontiers of this life."[17] The promotion of justice is, therefore, an integral part of evangelization.

31.   We are witnesses of a Gospel which links the love of God to the service of man, and that inseparably. In a world where the power of economic, social and political structures is now appreciated and the mechanisms and laws governing them are now understood, service according to the Gospel cannot dispense with a carefully planned effort to exert influence on those structures.

32.   We must bear in mind, however, that our efforts to promote justice and human freedom on the social and structural level, necessary though they are, are not sufficient of themselves. Injustice must be attacked at its roots which are in the human heart by transforming those attitudes and habits which beget injustice and foster the structures of oppression.

33.   Finally, if the promotion of justice is to attain its ultimate end, it should be carried out in such a way as to bring men and women to desire and to welcome the eschatological freedom and salvation offered to us by God in Christ. The methods we employ and the activities we undertake should express the spirit of the Beatitudes and bring people to a real reconciliation. In this way our commitment to justice will simultaneously show forth the spirit and the power of God. It will respond to humanity's deepest yearnings, not just for bread and freedom, but for God and His friendship—a longing to be sons and daughters in His sight.

34.   The initiatives required to respond to the challenges of our world thoroughly surpass our capabilities. Nonetheless we must set ourselves to the task with all the resourcefulness we have. By God's grace, a new apostolic awareness does seem to be taking shape

---

[16] Apoc. 21:1.

[17] Final Declaration of the Synod of Bishops of 1974, n. 12; see also the address of Pope Paul VI at the closing session of the Synod.

gradually in the Society as a whole. There is evidence of a widespread desire, and often of a whole-hearted effort, to renew and adapt our traditional apostolates and to embark on new ones. The guidelines that follow are meant to confirm or focus decisions and to urge us to more definite programs of action.

35. **Our involvement with the world.** Too often we are insulated from any real contact with unbelief and with the hard, everyday consequences of injustice and oppression. As a result we run the risk of not being able to hear the cry for the Gospel as it is addressed to us by the men and women of our time. A deeper involvement with others in the world will therefore be a decisive test of our faith, of our hope, and of our apostolic charity. Are we ready, with discernment and with reliance on a community which is alive and apostolic, to bear witness to the Gospel in the painful situations where our faith and our hope are tested by unbelief and injustice? Are we ready to give ourselves to the demanding and serious study of theology, philosophy and the human sciences, which are ever more necessary if we are to understand and try to resolve the problems of the world? To be involved in the world in this way is essential if we are to share our faith and our hope, and thus preach a Gospel that will respond to the needs and aspirations of our contemporaries.

36. New forms of apostolic involvement, adapted to different places, have already been developed. The success of these initiatives, whatever form they take, requires of us a solid formation, intense solidarity in community and a vivid awareness of our identity. Wherever we serve we must be attentive to "inculturation"; that is, we must take pains to adapt our preaching of the Gospel to the culture of the place so that men and women may receive Christ according to the distinctive character of each country, class or group and environment.

37. **Our collaboration with others.** The involvement we desire will be apostolic to the extent that it leads us to a closer collaboration with other members of the local churches, Christians of other denominations, believers of other religions, and all who hunger and thirst after justice; in short, with all who strive to make a world fit for men and women to live in, a world where brotherhood opens the way for the recognition and acceptance of Christ our Brother and

God our Father. Ecumenism will then become not just a particular ministry but an attitude of mind and a way of life. Today it is essential for the preaching and acceptance of the Gospel that this spirit of ecumenism embrace the whole of mankind, taking into account the cultural differences and the traditional spiritual values and hopes of all groups and peoples.

38. **The wellspring of our apostolate.** We are also led back again to our experience of the Spiritual Exercises. In them we are able continually to renew our faith and apostolic hope by experiencing again the love of God in Christ Jesus. We strengthen our commitment to be companions of Jesus in His mission, to labor like Him in solidarity with the poor and with Him for the establishment of the Kingdom. This same spiritual experience will teach us how to maintain the objectivity needed for a continuing review of our commitments. Thereby we gradually make our own that apostolic pedagogy of St. Ignatius which should characterize our every action.

❖ *Section C*

APOSTOLIC DECISIONS FOR TODAY

People and Structures

39. For the greater glory of God and salvation of men, Ignatius desired that his companions go wherever there was hope of the more universal good; go to those who have been abandoned; go to those who are in greatest need. But where is the greatest need today? Where are we to locate this hope for the more universal good?

40. It is becoming more and more evident that the structures of society are among the principal formative influences in our world, shaping people's ideas and feelings, shaping their most intimate desires and aspirations; in a word, shaping mankind itself. The struggle to transform these structures in the interest of the spiritual and material liberation of fellow human beings is intimately connected to the work of evangelization. This is not to say, of course,

that we can ever afford to neglect the direct apostolate to individuals, to those who are the victims of the injustice of social structures as well as to those who bear some responsibility or influence over them.

41.  From this point of view, desire for the more universal good is perfectly compatible with the determination to serve the most afflicted for the sake of the Gospel. Our preaching will be heard to the extent that witness accompanies it, the witness of commitment to the promotion of justice as an anticipation of the Kingdom which is to come.

### Social Involvement

42.  Our faith in Christ Jesus and our mission to proclaim the Gospel demand of us a commitment to promote justice and to enter into solidarity with the voiceless and the powerless. This commitment will move us seriously to verse ourselves in the complex problems which they face in their lives, then to identify and assume our own responsibilities to society.

43.  Our Jesuit communities have to help each of us overcome the reluctance, fear and apathy which block us from truly comprehending the social, economic and political problems which exist in our city or region or country, as well as on the international scene. Becoming really aware of and understanding these problems will help us see how to preach the Gospel better and how to work better with others in our own particular way without seeking to duplicate or compete with their strengths in the struggle to promote justice.

44.  We cannot be excused from making the most rigorous possible political and social analysis of our situation. This will require the utilization of the various sciences, sacred and profane, and of the various disciplines, speculative and practical, and all of this demands intense and specialized studies. Nothing should excuse us, either, from undertaking a searching discernment into our situation from the pastoral and apostolic point of view. From analysis and discernment will come committed action; from the experience of action will come insight into how to proceed further.

45.  In the discernment mentioned above, the local superior, and at times the provincial as well, will take part. This will help to overcome the tensions that arise and to maintain union of minds

and hearts. The superior will enable the members of the community not only to understand and appreciate the particular—and possibly unusual—apostolates undertaken by their companions under obedience, but also to take joint responsibility for them. And if contradictions arise as a result of a particular course of action, the community will be better prepared to "suffer persecution for justice's sake" if the decision to take that course has been prepared for by a discernment in which it had taken part or was at least represented by its superior.[18]

46. Any effort to promote justice will cost us something. Our cheerful readiness to pay the price will make our preaching of the Gospel more meaningful and its acceptance easier.

### Solidarity with the Poor

47. A decision in this direction will inevitably bring us to ask ourselves with whom we are identified and what our apostolic preferences are. For us, the promotion of justice is not one apostolic area among others, the "social apostolate"; rather, it should be the concern of our whole life and a dimension of all our apostolic endeavors.

48. Similarly, solidarity with men and women who live a life of hardship and who are victims of oppression cannot be the choice of a few Jesuits only. It should be a characteristic of the life of all of us as individuals and a characteristic of our communities and institutions as well. Alterations are called for in our manner and style of living so that the poverty to which we are vowed may identify us with the poor Christ, who identified Himself with the deprived.[19] The same questions need to be asked in a review of our institutions and apostolic works, and for the same reasons.

49. The personal backgrounds of most of us, the studies we make, and the circles in which we move often insulate us from poverty, and even from the simple life and its day-to-day concerns. We have access to skills and power which most people do not have. It will therefore be necessary for a larger number of us to share more

---

[18] See Matt. 5:10.

[19] See *SpEx*, 90, 147, 167; Matt. 25:35–45; also the decisions of the present General Congregation on poverty.

closely the lot of families who are of modest means, who make up the majority of every country, and who are often poor and oppressed. Relying on the unity we enjoy with one another in the Society and our opportunity to share in one another's experience, we must all acquire deeper sensitivity from those Jesuits who have chosen lives of closer approximation to the problems and aspirations of the deprived. Then we will learn to make our own their concerns as well as their preoccupations and their hopes. Only in this way will our solidarity with the poor gradually become a reality.

50.   If we have the patience and the humility and the courage to walk with the poor, we will learn from what they have to teach us what we can do to help them. Without this arduous journey, our efforts for the poor will have an effect just the opposite from what we intend and will only hinder them from getting a hearing for their real wants and from acquiring the means of taking charge of their own destiny, personal and collective. Through such humble service, we will have the opportunity to help them find, at the heart of their problems and their struggles, Jesus Christ living and acting through the power of the Spirit. Thus can we speak to them of God our Father who brings to Himself the human race in a communion of true brotherhood.

## The Service of Faith

51.   The life we lead, the faith-understanding we have of it and the personal relationship to Christ which should be at the heart of all we do are not three separate realities to which correspond three separate apostolates. To promote justice, to proclaim the faith and to lead others to a personal encounter with Christ are the three inseparable elements that make up the whole of our apostolate.

52.   We must therefore review not only our commitment to justice but our effectiveness in communicating the truths which give it meaning and in bringing men to find Christ in their daily lives. We must attentively examine our efforts to strengthen the faith of those who already believe in Christ, taking into account the formidable forces that in our time tend to undermine that faith. We must subject to a similarly searching examination our efforts to bring the Gospel to unbelievers (according to Decree 3 of the 31st General Congregation, especially n. 11).

53. In recent years the Church has been anxious to give fuller expression to her catholicity by paying more attention to the differences among her various members. More, perhaps, than in the past, she tries to take on the identity of nations and peoples, to align herself with their aspirations, both toward a socio-economic development and an understanding of the Christian mystery, in accord with their own history and traditions.

54. The incarnation of the Gospel in the life of the Church implies that the way in which Christ is preached and encountered will be different in different countries, different for people with different backgrounds. For some Christian communities, especially those in Asia and Africa, this "economy of the Incarnation" calls for a more intensive dialog with the heirs of the great non-Christian traditions. Jesuits working in these countries will have to take account of this. In some Western countries which can hardly be called Christian any longer, the language of theology and of prayer will also have to be suitably adapted. In those countries dominated by explicitly atheist ideologies, a renewed preaching of the Gospel demands not merely that our lives be, and be seen to be, in conformity with the commitment to justice Christ demands of us, but also that the structures of theological reflection, catechesis, liturgy and pastoral ministry be adapted to needs perceived through a real experience of the situation.

55. We are members of a Society with a universal vocation and a missionary tradition. We therefore have a special responsibility in this regard. We have a duty to ensure that our ministry is directed toward incarnating the faith and life of the Church in the culture and traditions of the people among whom and with whom we work and, at the same time, toward communion with all who share the same Christian faith.

56. Moreover, the Church is aware that today the problematic of inculturation must take into account not only the cultural values proper to each nation but also the new, more universal values emerging from the closer and more continuous interchange among nations in our time. Here, too, our Society is called upon to serve the Church; take part in her task of *aggiornamento,* of "bringing-up-to-date"; that is, of incarnating the Gospel in these values as well, these new values that are becoming increasingly planetary in scope.

## The Spiritual Exercises

57. The ministry of the Spiritual Exercises is of particular importance in this regard. A key element in the pedagogy of the Exercises is that its aim is to remove the barriers between God and man so that the Spirit speaks directly with man. Inherent in this Ignatian practice of spiritual direction is a deep respect for the exercitant as he is and for the culture, background and tradition that have gone into making him what he is. Moreover, the pedagogy of the Exercises is a pedagogy of discernment. It teaches a man to discover for himself where God is calling him, what God wants him to do, as he is, where he is, among his own people.

58. The Exercises also help to form Christians who, having personally experienced God as Savior, are able to stand back from the spurious absolutes of competing ideologies, and because of this detachment can play a constructive part in the reform of social and cultural structures. Thus, the ministry of the Spiritual Exercises is one of the most important we can undertake today. We should by all means encourage studies, research and experiment directed toward helping our contemporaries experience the vitality of the Exercises as adapted to the new needs which are theirs. Moreover the spirit of the Exercises should pervade every other ministry of the Word that we undertake.

## Guidelines for Concerted Action

59. In presenting this review of our apostolate in its various dimensions, the General Congregation wishes to continue along the lines given by Father General to the Congregation of Procurators of 1970* and to emphasize once more the importance of theological reflection, social action, education and the mass media as means of making our preaching of the Gospel more effective. The importance of these means rests in the fact that, in touching its most profound needs, they permit a more universal service to humankind.

60. In the concrete,

• We must be more aware of the need for research and for theological reflection, carried on in a context which is both interdis-

---

* [See the Yearbook of the Society of Jesus, 1971–1972.]

ciplinary and genuinely integrated with the culture in which it is done and with its traditions. Only thus can it throw light on the main problems which the Church and humanity ought to be coming to grips with today.

• Greater emphasis should be placed on the conscientization according to the Gospel of those who have the power to bring about social change, and a special place given to service of the poor and oppressed.

• We should pursue and intensify the work of formation in every sphere of education, while subjecting it at the same time to continual scrutiny. We must help prepare both young people and adults to live and labor for others and with others to build a more just world. Especially we should help form our Christian students in such a way that animated by a mature faith and personally devoted to Jesus Christ, they can find Him in others and having recognized Him there, they will serve Him in their neighbor. In this way we shall contribute to the formation of those who by a kind of multiplier-effect will share in the process of educating the world itself.

• We have to take a critical look at our ability to communicate our heart-felt convictions not only to persons we deal with directly, but also with those we cannot meet individually, and whom we can only help to the extent that we succeed in humanizing the social climate—attitudes and behavior—where we are engaged. In this regard the communications media would seem to play a role of great importance.

61. We should pursue these objectives not separately, in isolation, but as complementary factors of a single apostolic thrust toward the development of the whole person and of every person.

❖     *Section D*

# A MISSIONARY BODY

62.  The dispersal imposed on us today by our vocation as Jesuits makes it imperative that we strengthen and renew the ties that bind us together as members of the same Society.

63.  That is why it is so important that our communities be apostolic communities, and it is the primary responsibility of the local superior to see to it that his community approach this ideal as closely as possible. Each one of us should be able to find in his community in shared prayer, in converse with his brethren, in the celebration of the Eucharist the spiritual resources he needs for the apostolate. The community should also be able to provide him with a context favorable to apostolic discernment.

64.  It is this stress on the apostolic dimension of our communities that this 32nd General Congregation wishes to add to what the 31st General Congregation has already set forth in detail regarding the requirements of community life in the Society.[20] Our communities, even those whose members are engaged in different ministries, must have for their principle of unity the apostolic spirit.[21]

65.  It is important that whether a Jesuit works in a team or whether he works alone, he must be, and must feel himself to be, sent. It is the responsibility of the superior, after he has shared with the individual Jesuit in his discernment, to see to it that the apostolic work of each is properly integrated into the global mission of the Society. The individual Jesuit normally receives his mission

---

[20] GC 31, D. 19.

[21] See the directives of the present General Congregation in the document "The Union of Minds and Hearts," especially those regarding spiritual and community life.

from his provincial superior; but it belongs to the local superior to adapt that mission to local circumstances and to promote the sense of solidarity of the members of the community with each other and with the whole body of the Society to which they belong.

66. This solidarity with the Society is primary. It ought to take precedence over loyalties to any other sort of institution, Jesuit or non-Jesuit. It ought to stamp any other commitment which is thereby transformed into "mission." The "mission" as such is bestowed by the Society and is subject to her review. She can confirm or modify it as the greater service of God may require.

67. This kind of responsibility on the part of the superior cannot be exercised without the living practice of the account of conscience, by which the superior is made capable of taking part in the discernment done by each of the members and can help him therein.[22] It presupposes that, with the help of his companions, he engage in a continual, communitarian reflection upon fresh needs of the apostolate and upon the ways and means by which they can best be met. And it asks the superior to encourage the shy and the hesitant and to see to it that each individual finds a place in the community and a place in the apostolate which will bring out the best in him and enable him to cope with the hardships and risks he may encounter in God's service.

68. The apostolic body of the Society to which we belong should not be thought of just in terms of the local community. We belong to a province, which should itself constitute an apostolic community in which discernment and coordination of the apostolate on a larger scale than at the local level can and should take place. Moreover, the province is part of the whole Society, which also forms one single apostolic body and community. It is at this level that the over-all apostolic decisions and guidelines must be made and worked out, decisions and guidelines for which we should all feel jointly responsible.

69. This demands of all of us a high degree of availability and a real apostolic mobility in the service of the universal Church. Father General, with the help of his advisers, has the task of in-

---

[22] Ibid.

spiring the Society as a whole to serve the cause of the Gospel and
its justice. But we ask all our brothers, especially the provincials, to
give Father General all the support, all the ideas and assistance
which they can, as he tries to carry out this task of inspiring and
coordinating, even if this should shake up our settled habits or
stretch horizons sometimes all too limited. The extent to which our
contemporaries depend on one another in their outlook, aspirations
and religious concepts, to say nothing of structural connections that
span our planet, makes this over-all coordination of our efforts indispensable if we are to remain faithful to our mission of evangelization.

❖     *Section E*

## PRACTICAL DISPOSITIONS

70. The decisions and guidelines about our apostolic mission set
forth above have certain practical consequences which we now propose to detail in some points.

### A Program for Deepening Awareness and for Apostolic Discernment

71. Considering the variety of situations in which Jesuits are
working, the General Congregation cannot provide the programs
each region will need to reflect upon and implement the decisions
and guidelines presented here. Each province or group of provinces
must undertake a program of reflection and a review of our apostolates to discover what action is appropriate in each particular
context.

72. What is required is not so much a research program as a
process of reflection and evaluation inspired by the Ignatian tradition of spiritual discernment, in which the primary stress is on
prayer and the effort to attain "indifference," that is, an apostolic
readiness for anything.

73. The general method to be followed to produce this awareness and to engage in this discernment may be described (see *Octogesima Adveniens,* n. 4) as a constant interplay between experience, reflection, decision and action, in line with the Jesuit ideal of being "contemplative in action." The aim is to insure a change in our habitual patterns of thought, a conversion of heart as well as of spirit. The result will be effective apostolic decisions.

74. The process of evaluation and discernment must be brought to bear principally on the following: the identification and analysis of the problems involved in the service of faith and the promotion of justice and the review and renewal of our apostolic commitments. Where do we live? Where do we work? How? With whom? What really is our involvement with, dependence on, or commitment to ideologies and power centers? Is it only to the converted that we know how to preach Jesus Christ? These are some of the questions we should raise with reference to our membership individually, as well as to our communities and institutions.

## Continuing Evaluation of Our Apostolic Work

75. With regard to the choice of ministries and the setting up of priorities and programs, the General Congregation asks that the following guidelines be taken into account.

76. The review of our ministries and the deployment of our available manpower and resources must pay great attention to the role in the service of faith and the promotion of justice which can be played by our educational institutions, periodicals, parishes, retreat houses, and the other apostolic works for which we are responsible. Not only should our structured activities undergo this review, so should our individual apostolates.

77. In each province or region, or at least at the Assistancy level, there should be a definite mechanism for the review of our ministries.[23] Now is a good time to examine critically how these arrangements are working and, if need be, to replace them by others which are more effective and allow for a wider participation in the process of communal discernment. The appropriate major superior

---

[23] See GC 31, D. 22.

should make an annual report to Father General on what has been accomplished here.

## Some Special Cases

78.   The General Congregation recognizes how important it is that we should be present and work with others in different areas of human activity, especially in those parts of the world which are most secularized. It also recognizes the real opportunities for apostolic work afforded, in some cases, by the practice of a profession or by taking a job not directly related to the strictly presbyteral function.[24]

79.   The General Congregation considers that such commitments can be a part of the Society's mission, provided they meet the following conditions: They must be undertaken as a mission from our superiors. Their aim must be clearly apostolic. Preference should be given to work in an area which is de-Christianized or underprivileged. The activity must be in harmony with the priestly character of the Society as a whole. It must be compatible with the essential demands of the religious life—an interior life of prayer, a relationship with a Jesuit superior and a Jesuit community, poverty, apostolic availability.

80.   Any realistic plan to engage in the promotion of justice will mean some kind of involvement in civic activity. Exceptional forms of involvement must conform to the general practice of the Church[25] and the norms laid down by Father General.[26] If, in certain countries, it seems necessary to adopt more detailed norms and directives, this must be seen to by provincials—as far as possible in regional conferences. These norms and directives should be submitted to Father General for approval. It will then be for the provincial—with the agreement, where the case demands it, of the local bishop or the bishops' conference—to give or refuse the permission that may be required.

---

[24] See GC 31, D. 23, n. 12.

[25] See Synod of Bishops, 1971.

[26] *ActRSJ* 15:942.

## International Cooperation

81. All the major problems of our time have an international dimension. A real availability and openness to change will thus be necessary to foster the growth of cooperation and coordination throughout the whole Society. All Jesuits, but especially those who belong to the affluent world, should endeavor to work with those who form public opinion, as well as with international organizations, to promote justice among all peoples. To this end, the General Congregation asks Father General to make one or other of his advisers specifically responsible for the necessary organization of international cooperation within the Society, as required by our service of faith and promotion of justice.

# BIBLIOGRAPHY

*Acts of the Elective General Chapter of the Orders of Friars Preachers*. 1983. C. 14, no. [34] A.

Arrupe, Pedro, S.J. "Integration of Spiritual Life and Apostolate." *Acta Romana* 16, no. 4 (1976): 953–62.

———. "The Intellectual Apostolate in the Framework of the Society's Options Today." *Acta Romana* 16, no. 4 (1973–76): 996–1009.

———. "Letter on Apostolic Availability." *Acta Romana* 17, no. 1 (1977): 135–144.

———. "Men for Others." *Justice with Faith Today: Selected Lettters and Addresses–II,* 123–38. Ed. Jerome Aixala, S.J. St. Louis: Institute of Jesuit Sources, 1980.

———. *Rooted and Grounded in Love.* In *Documentation,* no. 47. Rome: Press and Information Office of the Society of Jesus, 1981.

Bartoletti et al. *Evangelizzazione e promozione umana: Riflessione biblico-teologico-pastorale.* Rome: Editrice AVE, 1976.

Calvez, Jean-Yves, S.J. "The Congregation and Closer Contact of Jesuits with Men." *Conferences on the Chief Decrees of the Jesuit General Congregation XXXII,* 147–61. St. Louis: The Institute of Jesuit Sources, 1976.

*Documents of the 31st and 32nd General Congregations of the Society of Jesus.* Ed. John W. Padberg, S.J. St. Louis: The Institute of Jesuit Sources, 1977.

*Documents of the 33rd General Congregation of the Society of Jesus.* St. Louis: Institute of Jesuit Sources, 1984.

*The Documents of Vatican II.* Ed. Walter M. Abbott, S.J. New York: Guild Press and America Press, 1966.

*Gaudium et spes* (*The Pastoral Constitution of the Church in the Modern World*). In *The Documents of Vatican II*, 199–308. Ed. Walter M. Abbott, S.J. New York: Guild Press and America Press, 1966.

General Chapter of the Society of the Divine Word. *The Promotion of Justice and Peace in Solidarity with the Poor in the Light of Constitution 112 II Directives on Poverty and Finances.* January 1983.

Gremillion, Joseph, ed. *The Gospel of Peace and Justice: Catholic Social Teaching since Pope John.* Maryknoll, New York: Orbis Books, 1976

Gutierrez Merino, Gustavo. *History, Politics, and Salvation.* Trans. and ed. Sister Caridad Inda and John Eagleson. Maryknoll, N.Y.: Orbis Books, 1973.

Ignatius of Loyola, Saint. *Epistolæ et instructiones.* 1st series, Monumenta Ignatiana. Vol. 22 of Monumenta Historica Societatis Iesu. Madrid, 1903; Rome, 1964. Vol. 1.

Janssens, John Baptist, S.J. "Instruction on the Social Apostolate." *Acta Romana* 11, no. 5 (1949): 709–26.

John XXIII, Pope. *Pacem in terris.* In *The Pope Speaks* 9, no. 1 (1963): 13–48.

John Paul II, Pope. *Dives in misericordia.* In *Origins* 10, no. 26 (Dec. 11, 1980): 401–16.

Lubac, Henri de, S.J. *La foi chrétienne.* Aubier, 1969.

Noble, H. D. "Introduction," *La charité.* Éditions de la *Revue des Jeunes,* 1969. Vol. 1.

*Our Mission Today: The Service of Faith and the Promotion of Justice, Decree Four of the Thirty-second General Congregation of the Society of Jesus.* In *Documents of the 31st and 32nd General Congregations of the Society of Jesus,* 411–38. Ed. John W. Padberg, S.J. St. Louis: The Institute of Jesuit Sources, 1977.

Paul VI, Pope. *Evangelii nuntiandi (On Evangelization in the Modern World)*. January 31, 1976. Daughters of St. Paul Edition.

———. *Ecclesiam suam*. In *The Pope Speaks* 10 (1964): 253–92.

———. *Octogesima adveniens*. In *The Gospel of Peace and Justice: Catholic Social Teaching since Pope John*, 485–512. Presented by Joseph Gremillion. Maryknoll, New York: Orbis Books, 1976.

Permanent Council of the French Episcopate. *Les libérations des hommes et le salut en Jésus-Christ*. Paris: Le Centurion, 1974.

Sobrino, Jon, S.J. "La promoción de la justicia come exigencia esencial del mensaje evangelico." *Diakonia*, no. 12 (December 1979).

*Societatis Iesu Constitutiones et Epitome Instituti*. Rome: General Curia of the Society of Jesus, 1962.

Synod of Bishops, 1971. *Justice in the World*. In *The Gospel of Peace and Justice: Catholic Social Teaching since Pope John*, 513–29. Presented by Joseph Gremillion. Maryknoll, New York: Orbis Books, 1976.

Thomas Aquinas, Saint. *Summa theologica*. Vol. 31. New York: McGraw–Hill Book Company, Blackfriars, 1974.